words *of* *a* feather

MURRAY SUID

Illustrations by Jeremy Eaton

New York Chicago San Francisco Lisbon London Madrid Mexico City
Milan New Delhi San Juan Seoul Singapore Sydney Toronto

The *McGraw-Hill* Companies

Library of Congress Cataloging-in-Publication Data

Suid, Murray I.
    Words of a feather : a humorous puzzlement of etymological pairs / by
Murray Suid.
        p.   cm.
    ISBN 0-07-147721-7
      1. English language—Etymology.   2. English language—Cognate words.
   3. English language—Roots.   I. Title.

    PE1574.S83   2006
    422—dc22   2006044855

2 3 4 5 6 7 8 9 10 11 12 13 14 15 16 17   DOC/DOC   0 9 8 7 6

ISBN-13: 978-0-07-147721-5
ISBN-10:   0-07-147721-7

Illustrations © 2007 by Jeremy Eaton

McGraw-Hill books are available at special quantity discounts to use as premiums
and sales promotions, or for use in corporate training programs. For more
information, please write to the Director of Special Sales, Professional Publishing,
McGraw-Hill, Two Penn Plaza, New York, NY 10121-2298. Or contact your local
bookstore.

This book is printed on acid-free paper.

This book is for my favorite flock:
Roberta, Anna, Devon, and Skylar.

Contents

Acknowledgments

I'm grateful to the many people who contributed to the making of this book. Special thanks go to: Carol Roth, my agent; Christian Bramswig, who pointed me toward several key resources; Carol Whiteley, who edited the proposal; Morag Martin, who provided a key piece of historical information; Holly McGuire, my editor; Marisa L'Heureux, who turned the manuscript into a book; and Roberta Suid, who provided thoughtful comments on each essay.

Introduction

What's the connection between *canary* and *canine*? How about between *appendix* and *penthouse*? *awesome* and *awful*? *bondage* and *husband*?

If these questions pique your interest, if they make you smile and speculate, then you're probably going to enjoy this collection of 150 linguistic riddles.

On each page you'll find a pair of words that trace back to a common ancestor. Such verbal relatives are called *doublets*. I can't remember when I first learned that they existed, but I know that I was fascinated. I thought that doublets were rarities, sort of like human twins, which—until in vitro fertilization—occurred about once in a hundred births.

In reality, doublets are common. There are thousands of them, tens of thousands. So the problem in making this book wasn't locating enough doublets to fill the pages but rather trying to select those that would have the greatest appeal. My scheme was to go for variety, looking for examples from many fields, including the performing arts (*ad-lib* and *libido*), economics (*affluence* and *influence*), science (*cosmos* and *cosmetics*), sports (*champion* and *champagne*), and religion (*God* and *gossip*).

I hope this collection holds your attention. But if you think you can come up with better examples, you're probably right. I encourage you to keep your eyes open and your notebook at the ready. Discovering a good doublet is thrilling, plus it enables you to entertain your friends or even strangers. Often when I was working on this project, I'd ask someone, "Hey, can you guess the relationship between *mortgage* and *mortuary*?" It's a real conversation starter.

You'll notice that a mini-essay accompanies each doublet. In a few hundred words, I trace the etymology of the pair back to a common ancestor, along the way often encountering words from Old English, French, German, Latin, and Greek.

No, I'm not a polyglot. I wish I were. I studied Latin once upon a time, but the main thing I remember is that I took it.

I admire professional etymologists—of whom there are more than you might guess—who can understand all those languages and who have the determination to spend months tracking down the biography of a word like *rigmarole*.

So if I'm not a linguist, where did I get the knowledge to write the texts accompanying each pair of words? I spent a lot of time paging through general dictionaries and etymological dictionaries, plus visiting some remarkable websites. I've listed these resources at the back of the book and commend them to you. Of course, any errors that made it into this volume are my responsibility.

I should add that research into word origins isn't boring even when it doesn't pan out, like the time I spent hours trying in vain to connect *drivel* with *dribble*. On the other hand, it's thrilling when a speculation pays off, as when *mailer-daemon* and *pande-*

monium came together. Before I started that particular investigation, I didn't even suspect that daemon programs existed. Word study often leads to that kind of unexpected discovery.

If you doubt what I'm saying about this sort of research, give it a go yourself. But watch out! You could be hooked trying to determine if *ballot* and *bullet* are an item or just passing acquaintances.

At the Back of This Book

At the back of the book you'll find the Word Factory, an overview of the ways in which words are created. Some of the methods likely are familiar, for example, compounding (*side* + *walk* = *sidewalk*) and imitating natural sounds (*buzz, bang, meow*). Other word-forming processes may be new to you, for example, metathesis, which means switching around letters (*dirt* was originally *drit*; *butterfly* came from the phrase *flutter by*).

Share and Share Alike

If you find mistakes in the text, or if you have questions, feel free to write me via the website: www.WordsofaFeather.net. Better yet, if this book inspires you to collect doublets and write about them, send them along. Who knows? Maybe you'll be able to contribute to *Words of a Feather*, Volume 2.

Words of a Feather

accordion & cordial

The first part of *accordion*—*accord*—is based on the Latin word *cor*, "heart," from which we get *coronary*, as in the phrase "coronary artery." *Accord* literally means "to the heart," suggesting the figurative meaning: "agreement," as when two bargaining entities announce: "We have finally reached an accord."

A further figurative meaning is "to harmonize," which inspired Cyrill Demian of Vienna—one of the many inventors of the accordion—to coin that name for the concertina-like device that he patented in 1829. (As with many Western contrivances, the starting point for the accordion goes back to a Chinese invention, but that's a different tale.)

The Latin *cor* also gives us *cordial*, which originally referred to anything that stimulated the heart in a positive manner, for example, food or drink. So when you sip a cordial—containing some form of alcohol, presumably—you're doing your heart a favor. Likewise, when you soothe the savage beast within by listening to harmonies played on the accordion, you might consider the music a "cordial." If it relaxes you, that's got to be beneficial.

Of course, not everyone loves the accordion. In his *Devil's Dictionary*, Ambrose Bierce sums up the naysayer's point of view with this definition: "Accordion, n. An instrument in harmony with the sentiments of an assassin."

acme & acne

In many dictionaries *acme* comes right before *acne*. This proximity suggests a link, and yet the words convey such different emotions: one up, one down.

Acme comes from the almost identical Greek *akme*, literally "the highest point"; figuratively "a peak experience." While we might use it in connection with life-altering events—getting into the college of our choice, winning the lottery, running a two-hour marathon, or meeting the person of our dreams—in reality we're more accustomed to encountering the term in business names such as *Acme Auto Wreckers*, *Acme Lock Security Center*, and *Acme Sanitation* (all from my local phone book, by the way).

Acne, on the other hand, is a despised skin disease characterized by chronic inflammation. For those who have suffered acne (that includes virtually all of us), the word connotes not peaks but the pits.

While these two words point in opposite directions, they actually have a strong etymological link. Indeed, they are as close to clones as words can be. In ancient Greece, because of the pimple's pointy shape, physicians at first used *acme* to refer to this malady. But while making a copy of a medical manuscript, an anonymous scribe accidentally wrote the Greek letter corresponding to our "n" instead of the one corresponding to our "m," thus creating *acne*, which is the form of the word that came to us, along with pimples, alas.

acrobat & acronym

The *acro* in *acrobat* comes to us from the Greek *akros*, whose primary meanings included "pointed" or "sharp." Metaphorically, perhaps inspired by pointy mountaintops, the word gained the additional meaning "high." This sense also gives us *acrophobia*, which the dictionary tells us is "an irrational fear of heights." Irrational, perhaps, but also common, afflicting about 10 percent of the population.

Acrobat's third syllable *bat* is also Greek, meaning "walk" or "go," which completes the picture of a performer crossing a wire high above the ground or swinging from a trapeze (named thus because of the trapezoidal shape made by the crossbar and the wires).

The *acro* in *acronym* relates to the idea that the point of something—for example, the point of an arrow—is located at its front end, the part that you first encounter. An acronym is a word formed from the first letter or letters of words in a phrase or even syllables in a word. For example, *scuba*, "equipment that allows divers to stay under water for longer than would be possible simply by holding their breath," comes from the first letters of words in the phrase "*s*elf-*c*ontained *u*nderwater *b*reathing *a*pparatus."

ad-lib & libido

No one knows for sure where the word *jazz* came from, but many etymologists speculate that it originally related to sexual activity.

Support for this hypothesis comes from an analysis of one of the key elements of jazz, *ad-libbing,* from the Latin phrase *ad libitum,* "at one's pleasure, as much as one likes."

Ad libitum in turn can be traced to the same root that gives us *libido,* Latin for "pleasure." Freud viewed libido as a form of psychic energy related to the sexual instinct.

Thus, it's not surprising that when comedians ad-lib their talk often deals with erotic subjects. A famous example is an exchange between Groucho Marx and a contestant on his 1950s comedy show "You Bet Your Life." Groucho asked, "Are you married?" The man replied, "Yes, we have eight kids." Groucho said, "How come eight?" The contestant answered, "I love my wife, and she loves kids, and so we had eight." At this point Groucho turned to the camera and said, "Well, I love my cigar, too, but I take it out of my mouth some of the time."

For Freud, the libido was a force that could be sublimated into creative activities, and ultimately was the engine for freedom. Understanding this, the authoritarian villains in George Lucas's *THX 1138* control the masses by criminalizing sexual intercourse. Everything is programmed. Nothing is left to chance. There is no improvisation. There is no jazz, sexual or otherwise.

adamant & diamond

When you're adamant about something, you're firm. Solid. Hard as a rock. Perhaps hard as a diamond. Which makes sense given the fact that the two words are from the same ancient source.

Adamant comes from *adamas*, a Greek compound made up of *a-*, "not," plus *damas*, "subdued, unbreakable." Figuratively, "resolute."

Diamond comes from the Old French *diamant*, "diamond," which again traces back to *adamas*. So a diamond is unbreakable, or at least, something that cannot be cut by anything else.

In a famous quotation, Winston Churchill sarcastically ridiculed the opposition party for being "Decided only to be undecided, resolved to be irresolute, adamant for drift," in other words "weak."

adjective & ejaculate

We can divide the world's population into two groups: those who are fascinated by grammar and those who aren't. This entry is for the three of us who constitute the grammar aficionados.

We're the kind of folks who appreciate knowing that *adjective* traces back to the Latin *adjectivus*, literally "thrown near," from the compound *ad*, "toward," plus *jacere*, "to throw." In the case of *adjective* this refers to a piece of information thrown at a noun to alter its meaning. For example, the adjective *humongous* will transform "my house" into "my humongous house"—that is, a mansion. Such a change may cause my neighbors to ejaculate a phrase like "Oh my!" or worse. Whether used to mean "to exclaim" or "to discharge (a bodily fluid)," *ejaculate* traces back to the Latin *e-*, "out," plus *jacere* (literally, "toss out").

While there's not much more to be said about ejaculation—at least not much more than we intend to say—many experts have denigrated the adjective, including Mark Twain—"As to the Adjective: when in doubt, strike it out"; Clifton Fadiman—"The adjective is the banana peel of the parts of speech"; and Ezra Pound—"Distrust adjectives."

The bible of the anti-adjective set is Strunk and White's *Elements of Style*, which states: "Write with nouns and verbs, not with adjectives and adverbs." As you can see, that sentence includes no adjectives and no adverbs. But if you analyze their entire book, you will discover that Strunk and White use about the same proportion of adjectives and adverbs as everyone else.

Which leads us to Lillian Hellman's counsel: "If I had to give young writers advice, I'd say don't listen to writers talking about writing."

adolescent & adult

You might think of *adolescent* and *adult* as antonyms, and at times they probably are. But etymologically these two words are closely connected, each deriving from the Latin *adolescere*, "to grow up," which traces back to the verb *alere*, "to nourish."

On the road to English, there was an etymological split. The present participle of *adolescere*—*adolescens*—means "growing up," and suggests a continuing process. Our word *adolescent* comes from this word, which makes sense because adolescents typically are works in progress.

Meanwhile, the past participle of *adolescere*—*adultus*—translates as "grown up," an action that is completed. This form, obviously, gave rise to *adult*. In theory, an adult may be labeled "mature," from the Latin *maturus*, "ripe." But which of us doesn't know at least one adult who could use a little more growing up?

Given that *adult*—in the phrase "adult movie"—has become a synonym for *pornographic* (from the Greek *porne*, literally "bought"), you might guess that *adultery* is etymologically related to *adult*. But in fact *adultery* derives from a completely different source, the Latin verb *adulterare*, "corrupt" or "make impure," which also gives us *adulterate*.

In other words, there is nothing *adult* about committing adultery—from the etymologist's point of view.

adversary & advertisement

Adversary traces back to the Latin *adversus*, "turned against." That's smart advice. An adversary is an enemy, someone who is against you, someone you don't turn away from . . . lest he shoot you in the back.

Advertisement comes from the same root. The operative concept is "turn." An advertisement turns you toward something: the seller's product or cause. In a sense, every advertisement calls out, "Hey, look over here, pay attention to me."

We know, of course, that not all advertisements have our best interests at heart. Therefore, the next time an advertisement tries to turn you around and tempt you to part with your purse, think of that paid-for message as your adversary. And if that's not enough to protect your money or your well-being, think of another Latin phrase: *caveat emptor* (buyer beware).

affluence & influence

The connection between wealth and power isn't news. More than two thousand years ago, a freed slave Publilius Syrus wrote: "Money alone sets all the world in motion."

How appropriate, then, that there is a strong etymological link between *affluence* and *influence*. The former comes from the Latin *affluere*, literally "flow toward," which hints at the idea of wealth flowing to a lucky person, or in today's idiom, "positive cash flow."

The etymology of *influence* is almost identical. The Latin *influere* means literally "flow into." But there is a detour in our story. Originally, the word was used astrologically to describe power that flowed from the stars and controlled a person's destiny.

In the centuries that followed, *influence* came to refer to the effect of nonastronomical forces such as alcohol ("under the influence") and germs (*influenza*, later clipped to *flu*) and, especially, financial power.

While many have spoken negatively about the rich ("If all the rich men in the world divided up their money amongst themselves, there wouldn't be enough to go around."—novelist Christina Stead), we found only one authority who observed a case in which money had no influence. Comtesse De Voigrand wrote: "There are poor men in this country who cannot be bought: the day I found that out, I sent my gold abroad."

aghast & ghost

When you're aghast—perhaps because you see something ghastly—you're frightened, even horrified. It's as if you've seen a ghost. Which is as it should be, because *aghast* and the related *ghastly* derive from the Old English word *gast*, meaning "ghost."

The *a* in *aghast* belongs to the category of words and syllables known as "intensives." They add force or emphasis to a word or phrase. A familiar example is the use of "very" in the expression "the very thought of it." In the present case, when you're aghast, you're REALLY frightened.

Back to *ghost*: originally, the word referred to the soul or spirit, a usage familiar in the religious phrase "Holy Ghost." Nothing upsetting in that sense of the word.

It wasn't until the fourteenth century that *ghost* began to acquire the contemporary meaning of "a life-like dead person out to scare or warn the living." This led to the invention of the ghost in literature, such as the specter of Hamlet's father. Ghost stories became enormously popular in the nineteenth century, the most enduring example being Dickens' *A Christmas Carol*.

Exactly why people plunk down money for the privilege of being frightened is worth pondering. Perhaps the journalist Ed Howe got it right when he wrote: "A good scare is worth more to a man than good advice."

Or maybe it has something to do with the fact that in a recent poll, half the people in the United States believe that ghosts exist, a scary thought whether you agree with that part of the population or not.

agony & antagonist

Vinko Bogataj is not a household name. But his spectacular fall at the International Ski Flying Championship in 1970 made "agony of defeat" into one of the best-known phrases in English.

The etymology of *defeat* is straightforward; it comes from the Latin *diffacere*, "not perform." Watching Vinko miss his landing is to understand at the deepest level the idea of not performing. (Those of you who have seen the opening clip on "Wide World of Sports" will be happy to know that Vinko survived and went on to become a coach.)

Agony has a more subtle etymology. Although for centuries the word has meant mental and bodily suffering, its Greek source—*agon*—actually refers to the contest or struggle itself. The *ant-* in *antagonist* means "against," so that the antagonist is the person or thing you struggle against.

Thus, *agony* is about struggle and not—as the "agony of defeat" seems to imply—about the pain resulting from a defeat.

All of this suggests that the great Super Bowl–winning coach Vince Lombardi might have misled us with his assertion that "Winning isn't everything; it's the only thing." From the etymological perspective, the game is what matters most. An amateur running in a marathon may experience great agony yet not give a fig about winning or losing.

But of course, so far as I have been able to determine, no etymologist has ever won a Super Bowl—or, like Mr. Lombardi, had a trophy named for him or her.

alderman & auld lang syne

Sometimes voters feel like booting out the old guard and bringing in young blood. Whether or not this is politically wise, it's etymologically questionable if the election involves a city council made up of aldermen. That's because *alderman* comes to us from the Middle English *ealdorman*, whose first syllable *eald* meant "aged" or "old." If you get rid of the old men, linguistically you won't have any *aldermen* left.

You can detect the same root in the phrase "elder statesman." So to talk about a "youthful alderman" or "fresh-faced elder statesman" doesn't make a lot of verbal sense.

The syllable *eald* is a relative of the Scottish word *auld*, "old," as in the song, "Auld Lang Syne," literally "old long since," in other words, "the good old days," the days when politicians were to be trusted. (In your dreams.)

ale & aluminum

Since the later decades of the twentieth century, ale has been sold in aluminum cans. That packaging decision by ale manufacturers has been a huge success. But there's a more historic connection between ale and aluminum.

Although its etymology is not certain, the word *ale* appears to derive from the Latin *alumen*, "alum," literally "bitter salt." Most people who have sipped ale will probably understand the appropriateness of that name.

Aluminum comes from the exact same Latin source, probably because the earliest knowledge of this element was in the form of aluminum salt—alum. The ancient Greeks and Romans used this substance in the dyeing process and also to stop the flow of blood from minor cuts.

In 1812 Sir Humphry Davy, who was among the first to recognize that aluminum was an element, labeled the substance *aluminum*, the name that took hold in the United States. However, in England another British scientist persuaded the scientific community to change the name to *aluminium*, following the "ium" pattern of other elements that Davy had discovered, including potassium and calcium.

Aluminium eventually became the preferred form of the word in most places around the world. But in the United States scientists and lay people alike stayed with the spelling proposed by the man who coined the word.

alias & alibi

Two items that experienced criminals find handy are aliases and alibis. Fortunately, these can be found at the same place—etymologically speaking.

Alias comes from the Latin *alius*, "other." By assuming some other identity, the bad guy hopes to avoid arrest. So for example, Jesse James called himself "Mr. Howard." Unfortunately, his face gave him away.

When an alias doesn't work, the criminal—if still alive—will try to escape the mess by using an alibi. In Latin, a noun could take the locative form, indicating place, just as the possessive form in English indicates ownership. *Alibi* is the locative form of *alius* with the sense of "elsewhere." If you're in some other place, you couldn't have been at the scene of the crime and hence are innocent.

Not that they're criminals, but some writers and actors employ aliases—pseudonyms and stage names. We can identify at least three reasons that artists give themselves fake names:

- to simplify: Edda Kathleen van Heemstra calling herself "Audrey Hepburn"
- to gain attention: Arnold Dorsey calling himself "Engelbert Humperdink" (a name borrowed from a German composer of operas)
- to hide one's roots: Jacob Cohen calling himself "Rodney Dangerfield"

alimony & alimentary canal

Pillsbury's famous slogan—"Nothing says lovin' like something from the oven"—suggests a tie between romance and rations. Whether or not that bit of doggerel is true, there's evidence that even after love dies, even after matrimony has been put asunder, food still links ex-partners. We're speaking of course of alimony.

Alimony comes from the Latin *alere*, to nourish. This same ancient word gives us *alimentary*, "related to food," most commonly used in the phrase "alimentary canal," which begins, romantically enough, at the kisser, and ends . . . at the other end.

We should note that the final part of alimony—*mony*—does not relate to money even though alimony usually involves the payment of money. Rather, *-mony* is a suffix that refers to "the means of accomplishing something," for example, supporting a former spouse. It also means "a state of being," for example . . . *matrimony*. But isn't this where we came in?

amble & ambulance

When you need an ambulance, there's a good chance that you can't get along under your own power. It may seem ironic, therefore, that the word *ambulance* comes through French from the Latin *ambulare*, "to walk," which also gives us *amble*, "to walk in a leisurely fashion." But how are you going to walk at any pace if you're injured?

This linguistic mystery is resolved when we learn that *ambulance* was first used metaphorically as the name of a movable field hospital used by the French military in the seventeenth century. The modern equivalent would be the "Mobile Army Surgical Hospital" (MASH) made famous in the film by Robert Altman and the television program based on it.

By the nineteenth century, *ambulance* was the name given to vehicles that transported the sick and injured to permanent hospitals. The "engines" for these conveyances of mercy could be horses or even people—one hopes moving at a rate that was faster than what *amble* currently connotes. But then again, in a traffic jam, even a modern ambulance might find the going slow enough to accurately reflect its etymological root.

amicable & enemy

Those of us who studied Latin may not remember much, but we will never forget the conjugation of the verb *amare*: *amo*, "I love;" *amas*, "you love"; *amat*, "he or she loves." We recognize the root in the 1953 hit "That's Amore" sung by the late crooner Dean Martin.

From *amare* the English language got *amateur*, a soon-to-be-obsolete label for a person who does something out of love for the activity and not for money.

The same source also gave us two adjectives—*amiable* and *amicable*—that like fraternal twins are similar yet different.

Amiable, which is closer to its roots, means "lovable" or "having a good nature." *Amicable*, which is a few degrees less warm, means "showing good will" and is used most often in the phrase "amicable divorce."

Which brings us to *enemy*. Love and friendship reside in this word, but their presence is disguised by a prefix and by spelling. *Enemy* comes to us from the Old French *enemi*, which comes from the Latin *inimicus*, a compound of *en-*, "not" and *amicus*, "friend," which of course comes from *amare*.

Philosophers have long explored the relationship between friends and enemies. For example, William Blake wrote: "It is easier to forgive an enemy than to forgive a friend."

But let's give the last word to the comedian Eddie Cantor: "He hasn't an enemy in the world—but all his friends hate him."

Ammon & ammonia

To appreciate this entry, you need to know about Ammon. If you can already identify him, please go directly to paragraph 3.

Once upon a time, Ammon was the top god in Egyptian mythology. Later he was borrowed by the Greeks and renamed "Zeus." The Romans called him "Jupiter." By any name, he was powerful, at least in the minds of those who worshipped him.

You might wonder, "What does such a high and mighty being—even one that's mythical—have to do with ammonia, a compound used to make cleaning agents, fertilizers, and plastics?" The story is a pisser, literally.

Around five thousand years ago, when pilgrims came to pay homage to Ammon at his temple in Thebes, they tied their camels nearby, the way cowboys parked their horses outside a saloon. Camels, doing what mammals do, urinated on the spot, where it soaked deeply into the desert sand. Lots of camels, lots of urine. Probably some folks were put off by the smell. But an enterprising businessperson used the sands to produce a cleaning agent known—in Egyptian—as "salt of Ammon."

Centuries later Pliny the Elder mentioned the substance, which he called *Hammoniacus sal*. In the middle ages, dyers used ammonia, again made from urine, to produce their dyes. In the eighteenth century, a Swedish chemist coined the modern form of the word from the Greek *ammoniakon*, "belonging to Ammon."

In the early part of the twentieth century, Fritz Haber developed a method for producing large quantities of ammonia from nitrogen in the air. This led to the use of ammonia in the manufacture of munitions during World War I. The resulting big explosions, more than household cleaning products, might have gotten the approval of a powerful god like Ammon.

analgesic & nostalgia

Anything that stops or limits pain may be called an *analgesic*, from the Greek *an-*, "against," plus *algos*, "pain." Pain remedies are by far the best-selling over-the-counter drugs.

Here then is the paradox: Huge numbers of people gladly suffer nostalgia. A web search on this affliction turned up 23 million sites, most of them promoting nostalgia, for example, by offering "Oldies but Goodies." Yet nostalgia, once classified as an actual disease, is a compound of the Greek *nostos*, "homecoming," plus our old enemy *algos*, "pain." Why would people be drawn to the painful experience of nostalgia? A poem by Tennyson gives us a clue as to why such pain is attractive:

> *Tears, idle tears, I know not what they mean,*
> *Tears from the depth of some divine despair*
> *Rise in the heart and gather to the eyes,*
> *In looking on the happy autumn-fields,*
> *And thinking of the days that are not more.*

In a note about his poem, Tennyson explained: "It is what I have always felt even from a boy, and what as a boy I called the 'passion of the past.' And it is so always with me now; it is the distance that charms me in the landscape, the picture and the past, and not the immediate today in which I move."

Could it be that the masses—and not just the poets—use the past, even an imaginary version of the past, as an antidote for the pain of the present? If so, nostalgia might be understood as a self-prescribed drug, one that carries a high risk of addiction.

anecdote & antidote

Anecdote and *antidote* are alike in two ways. First, they're both meant as cures, the former for boredom, the latter for poison. Second, they share the same verbal root.

Antidote comes from the Greek *anti-*, "against," plus *didonai*, "to give." Literally, the word means "to give against"; the figurative sense is "to give something against an agent causing illness." From the ending *donai* we get the words *dose*, *dosage*, and *donate*.

Anecdote goes back first to the Greek *anekdotos*, *an-*, "not," plus *ekdotos*, "published." Literally, "unpublished work." This doesn't look much like a donation until we split *ekdotos* into its parts: *ek*, "out," plus *didonai*, which we already learned is "to give." In other words, for the Greeks, *publishing* meant "giving out."

The word *anekdotos* was first used in a specific instance, as the title of Procopius's unpublished memoirs of Emperor Justinian I. Of course, like most secret memoirs, the book eventually was "given out" and its juicy gossip ultimately gave *anecdote* its meaning of an entertaining and true story.

anger & angina

We hear a lot about how bad cholesterol contributes to heart disease. And maybe it does. But Dr. Etymology suggests another cause and a possible remedy.

Let's start with *angina*, from the ancient Greek *ankhone*, "a strangling." When combined with the Latin *pectus*, "breast," we get *angina pectoris*, chest pain caused by a sudden decrease of the blood supply to the heart muscle. The malfunctioning blood vessels strangle the heart.

Now what has this to do with anger? *Anger* comes to us after a long etymological journey that starts with the Old Norwegian *angra*, "vex," which goes back further to the Old English *enge*, "narrow," which goes back even further to the Greek *ankhein*, "to squeeze," which—as you might guess—is a close relative of the word we met earlier, *ankhone*, "a strangling."

Clearly, the dictionary is telling us that anger leads to the kind of tightness, narrowing, and squeezing that ultimately shuts off circulation and leads to anguish, "pain," from the same root that gives us *angina*.

What to do? Smile. Be happy. And remember what Samuel Goldwyn is alleged to have said: "This makes me so sore it gets my dandruff up."

animal & animation

According to legend, motion picture technology was invented to settle a bet by Leland Stanford, the railroad magnate who served as California's eighth governor and who also cofounded Stanford University. At issue was whether or not a trotting horse ever has all four feet off the ground at the same time. In 1874, doing research funded by Stanford, Eadweard Muybridge settled the question—yes, horses do "fly"—and simultaneously showed the world how to make movies.

Decades later, when Ub Iwerk, Walt Disney, and others perfected the animated cartoon, like Muybridge, they chose animals for their subjects, turning rodents, ducks, pigs, birds, coyotes, and other creatures into overnight stars. Casting animals was a proper decision not only in terms of box office but also from the etymological perspective.

Animal comes from the Latin *anima*, literally "breath" and figuratively "life" as in the Biblical passage: "And the Lord God formed man of the dust of the ground, and breathed into his nostrils the breath of life; and man became a living being."

In English, *animal* was a rival term for *beast* and didn't become a popular word until the Elizabethan era. But it was well established by the nineteenth century, when the phrase "animal rights" came into use.

Animation derives from the Latin verb *animare*, "to give breath to," which of course goes right back to *anima*. So an animator is, in a way, a god-like figure, breathing life into a series of still pictures.

animal & animation

apocryphal & crypt

Synonyms for *apocryphal* include *dubious* and *untrue*, adjectives used to denounce urban legends and misleading information. But once upon a time, *apocryphal* had a positive, even mystical meaning. How then did the sense of the word turn negative? With a little digging, we should be able to uncover the facts.

Apocryphal comes from the Greek *apokruphos*, whose root *kruptein* means "to hide." The same word is the source of *crypt*, "a hidden burial place," best known in our time as part of the title of a popular movie and television program, both based on the "Tales from the Crypt" comic book series. The same Greek root gave rise to the word *cryptography*, "a method of writing that hides the meaning of a message."

In the years following the death of Jesus, *apocryphal* was applied to religious writings that were considered by some to be too sacred and important to share with the masses. To enhance the mystery, the authorship of these writings was kept secret.

Centuries later, when church leaders came to the conclusion that ideas in the apocrypha endangered the teachings of the approved Biblical texts, the leaders condemned the apocrypha as being false and heretical. In so doing, they changed the meaning of *apocrypha* from "secret" and "mysterious" to false and evil.

This negative meaning stayed with *apocryphal* even after the term came to be used with nonreligious texts. As Ben Franklin explained, "Glass, china, and reputation are easily cracked, and never mended." Ben was, of course, thinking of people, but his point is valid also for the reputation of words.

appendix & penthouse

A penthouse is obviously not a house. Nor—despite the syllable *pent*, which might make us think of *five*, as in *pentagon*—does a penthouse have to be on the fifth floor. So how do we explain the puzzling components of this word for an apartment built on the roof of a building?

The answer is "folk etymology," a ubiquitous word-making process by which sounds in unfamiliar words are transformed into familiar sounds that are easier to remember. For example *mayday*, the call for help, is the English rendition of the French "m'aider." The word has nothing to do with the month of May. Folk etymology occurs even within a language, as when a person unfamiliar with air ducts turns "duct tape" into "duck tape."

And *penthouse*? The word comes from the Old French *apentis*, which referred to "something attached." This meaning is found in the closely related *appendix*. We might go back further to the Latin *pendere*, the source of *pendulum* and *pending*.

But our concern here is *apentis*. After *apentis* was imported into England during the Norman era, it was clipped to *pentis*. Because the word referred to a structure often used as a living space, the Anglo-Saxons came to pronounce *pentis*'s final syllable *is* as "house" and then spell it that way. (Say the word five times quickly and you may understand the transformation.)

Because a penthouse isn't a lean-to but rather an apartment atop a building, one might question the validity of calling that thing a "house." But language is conservative, and as Gertrude Stein might have written: A house is a house is a house. And then, too, if someone shells out ten million dollars for the thing, maybe they ought to have the right to call it whatever they like.

apron & napkin

Apron and *napkin* are obviously connected in terms of functionality, referring to objects that protect us from food handling sloppiness. The two words are also closely connected etymologically. But the link isn't apparent, ironically because of pronunciation sloppiness. Here are the messy facts.

Apron traces back to the Old French *naperon*, "cloth." It was borrowed into Middle English as a *napron*. If you lived in the thirteenth century and wanted to protect your clothes while cooking and if you had the resources to do so, you would wear "a napron."

But if you say "a napron" quickly and repeatedly, it sometimes sounds like "an apron," and eventually that's how the phrase came to be pronounced and later spelled.

As for napkin, it too goes back to the Old French *nappe*, "cloth," but the diminutive ending *-kin* turned the word into "a little cloth," that is, the kind of small protective cloth diners might place in their laps or tuck into their shirts. (Why, following the same process, the phrase "a napkin" didn't become "an apkin" is one of those quirks that make language so interesting.)

Other examples of words created by mispronunciation—technically known as "misdivision"—include "an auger," which originally was "a nauger," and "a newt," which originally was "an ewte."

Don't think that this process happens only among ancient and illiterate people. A modern example is the widely used expression "a nother thing."

assassin & hashish

"O God," wrote Shakespeare, "that men should put an enemy in their mouths to steal away their brains!" The poet was referring to the way that alcohol kills a person's ability to think clearly, a charge that might be leveled against any narcotic.

So, using poetic license, we might link *hashish* and *assassin* by arguing that hashish assassinates higher brain function. But in truth, the link between the two words is more prosaic than that.

In 1300, armed thugs in Turkey often hired themselves out as paid murderers. Before doing their dastardly deeds, they would sometimes smoke hashish either to build their courage or dull their morality or perhaps simply to have a good time.

In any case, as alcoholics are so named for the alcohol that is their drug of choice, those early rented killers were named for their favorite drug, hashish, and thus were known as *hashhashans*, "hash eaters." To English ears, *hashhashans* sounded like "assassins."

attraction & tractor-trailer

The root *trahere* is found in many English words, including *contract*, *extract*, *subtract*, *traction*, and *tractor-trailer*, a tractor used to pull a trailer or a wagon. These days, the more common name is a *big rig* or, in England, a *lorry*. But whatever it's called, the tractor provides the moving power.

From *trahere*, we also get *attraction*, the sense being to pull one thing to another thing as, for example, a magnet pulls a piece of iron to itself. Through metaphorical extension, *attraction* acquired the meaning of "personal appeal" in the early seventeenth century. By the middle of the nineteenth century, this meaning was also applied to inanimate objects, for example, an attractive hotel.

In the early 1920s, this use of the word gave rise to the advertising phrase "Preview of Coming Attractions." Movie insiders called such previews *trailers* because originally they trailed the feature. When the exhibitors realized that audiences often departed at the end of the feature and before the trailers did their work, the trailers were moved to the head of the program. But given the inherent conservative nature of language—think of how we still call eyeglasses "glasses" even though the lenses frequently are made of plastic—*trailer* is still the term used in the industry.

There's one more beat to this etymology if you'll permit yourself to be dragged along. The word *trailer* came into English from the Latin *tragula*, "dragnet," which some authorities believe relates to our old pal *trahere*, "to pull." Although this doesn't seem to fit the sort of passive trailer found in a trailer park, when you think of how a movie trailer pulls in business, perhaps the word does have some of those *trahere* genes.

automobile & mob

Invented to democratize transportation—a horse or even hundreds of horses in every garage—the *automobile* (a compound based on the Greek *auto*, "self," plus the Latin *mobilis*, "movable") has had numerous unintended consequences. Most of us can recite them automatically: polluting the air, despoiling farmland, contributing to global warming, killing thousands of innocent victims, and putting millions of commuters into virtual solitary confinement.

That last byproduct—isolation—raises a question: What's the link between such an antisocial conveyance and something as gregarious as a mob?

The answer starts with *mob*, which is clipped from a Late Latin phrase *mobile vulgus*, "moving crowd." In the seventeenth century, when the common folk assembled for a protest, because they were not yet protected by a constitutional right to assemble peaceably, they roamed the streets, keeping one step ahead of the authorities.

By the early nineteenth century, *mob* had come to mean a crowd with a criminal intent, such as a gang of pickpockets, on the move for obvious reasons. Then in the early twentieth century, the word was applied to organized criminal groups—The Mob.

Now that a mob might operate out of a fixed place—like Tony Soprano's Bada Bing—the word has lost the sense of mobility (sort of like high-powered automobiles stuck in traffic jams—going nowhere fast).

awesome & awful

These days, *awesome* and *awful* are antonyms, the former meaning "splendid" and "astounding," the later meaning "horrible" and "rotten." But a few centuries ago, *awesome* and *awful* were synonyms.

Both, of course, are based on *awe*, which comes to English from the Old Norse *agi*, "fright, terror," which etymologists trace back to a hypothetical ancient German word, *agis*, "fear."

The word's use in Biblical texts—such as "Princes have persecuted me without a cause: but my heart standeth in *awe* of thy word" (Psalm 119)—added the sense of respect and wonder. Thus *awe* could consist of a medley of emotions, such as what was felt by those observing the detonation of the first atom bomb.

By the sixteenth century, *awesome* came to mean "good" in everyday contexts, and it has remained positive over the centuries, while losing most of its spiritual connotations.

Meanwhile, *awful* went in a completely different direction. While it retained its positive sense up to the mid-nineteenth century—for example in Lord Tennyson's line "God made Himself an awful rose of dawn"—by the early twentieth century, it was used negatively, as in this J. C. Johnson blues lyric made famous by Bessie Smith:

> *When my bed get empty,*
> *Make me feel awful mean and blue.*

More often it conveyed the sense that something was bad in the extreme as when Britain's King George V said: "Is it possible that my people live in such awful conditions? . . . I tell you, Mr. Wheatley, that if I had to live in conditions like that I would be a revolutionary myself."

bankrupt & banquet

Henry Ford once remarked: "It is well enough that the people of this nation do not understand our banking and monetary system, for if they did, I believe there would be a revolution before tomorrow morning."

Mindful of the consequences of launching a revolution, in this entry we will not help you understand the banking and monetary system. But we will take the risk of helping you grasp the etymologies of *bankrupt* and *banquet*.

Let's start with the first syllable of *bankrupt*. Although the idea of banking goes back for millennia, the word *bank* is relatively recent, coming into English in the fifteenth century from the Old Italian *banca*, "bench." In the middle ages, individual money-lenders—the original bankers—conducted their business on benches outdoors.

Bankruptcy's second syllable—*rupt*—comes from the Latin *rupta*, "broken." Literally, it meant "broken bench," figuratively, the end of one's business.

It's easy to imagine a logical connection between *bankrupt* and *banquet*. If you're a spendthrift—wasting your money on frivolities, such as banquets—of course you'll run out of money and go bankrupt, unless you're living in the Middle Ages when a banquet was, in Old Italian *banchetto*, "little bench," figuratively a modest repast eaten on a bench. This was a far cry from today's grandiose banquets, but of course back then they didn't have credit cards.

bedlam & Bethlehem

Synonyms for *bedlam* include *chaos*, *devastation*, and *destruction*.

These same words often could be applied to *Bethlehem*, the Middle East town that has been a battleground for at least two thousand years. After Jesus' birth, Herod condemned to death all the children under two living in and near Bethlehem. The city was destroyed in Bar Kokhba's revolt a century later, then sacked in the Samaritan revolt five centuries later, then invaded by the Persians . . . then by the Crusaders . . . then . . .

You get the picture. But although *Bethlehem* is in fact the source of *bedlam*, the etymology leads us not to the Middle East, but rather to London.

In 1247, a religious organization in London decided to name their new priory *Bethlehem*. This seems like an appropriate choice, given that the word traces back to a Hebrew compound *beth lehem*, literally "house of bread," figuratively "a place to nurture the body and the soul."

A few decades later, the building was converted to the "Hospital of Saint Mary of Bethlehem." And then in 1402 it became an asylum for "lunatics" and was called simply "Bethlehem."

In those days before modern psychiatric care—and Prozac—turmoil was no stranger to such asylums. By 1667, through the etymological process known as "colloquial pronunciation," *Bethlehem* had been transformed into *bedlam*.

Before we spill too much contempt upon the caregivers of the Bethlehem asylum, let us recall that the movie *One Flew over the Cuckoo's Nest* tells a story about a loony bin of our era's design.

blog & log

Like many blended words—such as *smog* (from *smoke* plus *fog*)—the immediate origin of *blog* is quite apparent. *Blog* was coined in the 1990s from *web* plus *log* to name a website devoted to an online diary.

This could be the end of the entry, but authors—at least this one—generally like to fill up their pages. Moreover, the above spare etymology leads to some surprising connections if we travel on just a bit.

Web comes from the Old English *webb*, "woven material." Given that this is a word book, we should add that the family name *Webster* original meant a "weaver."

In the thirteenth century, by metaphorical extension, *web* came to refer to a spider's construction. Seven hundred years after that, *web* was extended again to refer to a collection of computers woven together into a digital network.

And *log*? Although its ultimate origin is unknown, we do know how it came to be used in the sense of "journal." As with one of the earliest computing terms—*cybernetics*, from a Greek word meaning "helmsman"—*log* entered digital speak from seafarers' jargon. More than seven centuries before the log kept by the captain of the Starship *Enterprise*, sailors recorded the details of their voyages in a *logbook*, so named because the ship's speed was calculated by how quickly it moved past a log floating in the water.

How simple things used to be.

bondage & husband

This entry may not be what you expect. But the heading was too good to pass up, and it's accurate: *husband* and *bondage* are two words of a feather.

Husband comes from the Old English *husbonda*, meaning (at that time!) "master of a house, one who manages resources economically." The first syllable of the word—*hus*—was the Old English word for "house." The same word is found in the ancient *huswif*, "housewife," which eventually came to be pronounced "huzzy" and spelled *hussy*, with the disrespectful meaning of a loose woman.

Back to *husband*, which also suffered a downward semantic slide: The second syllable, *band*, is from the Old English *bonda*, "a farmer," which originally was a respectable calling. But after the Norman Conquest in 1066, the word came to name someone under the control of the lord of the manor. Hence, *bonda* signified subjection, from which arose the word *bondage*.

Happily, with the rise of democratic institutions and the decline of the power of the lords, husbands are no longer seen as suffering in bondage, except perhaps in tasteless jokes.

bus & omniscient

Imagine a group of ancient Roman tourists transported by time machine to a modern metropolis. Of all the innovations they'd see, the one that might astound them most is the word *bus*. Not the vehicle, the word.

The Romans would recognize the sound of the syllable, but would have no clue how *bus* came to name that big noisy conveyance because in Latin, *bus* is not a noun and doesn't refer to anything. In case you meet one of those time-traveling visitors, here's the story.

We start with the French expression *voiture omnibus*; *voiture* is French for "carriage" while *omnibus* is Latin, "for all." Thus *voiture omnibus* is a vehicle meant to carry all the people.

Omnibus is from the Latin root *omnis*, "all," found in many English words such as *omniscient*, "knowing all," *omnipotent*, "being all powerful," *omnipresent*, "being in all places," and *omnivorous*, "eating everything."

The last syllable of *omnibus*—*bus*—is simply a suffix meaning "for." In Latin *-bus* can no more stand alone than can the English possessive suffix *'s*, meaning "of." By itself *'s* has no meaning.

When *voiture omnibus* entered English, *voiture* was dropped, leaving *omnibus* as the name for the mass-transit vehicle. *Omnibus* was also the name of a 1950s TV show that was "for all the people."

Eventually—some linguists might say "illogically"—the *omni-* part of *omnibus* was clipped, leaving the "meaningless" syllable *bus* as the name for a land-based mass-transit vehicle, the name of an airplane manufacturer (Airbus)—and even a circuit carrying information to and from digital machines.

Bus, we can say, has come a long way from its roots.

cabbage & captain

Old English was the source of many modern body part names: *eare*, "ear," *ege*, "eye," *fot*, "foot," *hond*, "hand," *lippa*, "lip," *nosu*, "nose," *tonge*, "tongue," and *arse* (not a euphemism, by the way, but the original form of the word).

Body part words have frequently been used in new ways: *elbow* your way into line, *finger* the guilty party, *back* of a chair, *heart* of the matter, *tongue* of a shoe, *lip* of a cup, *nosecone*, *eyelet*, and *handout*.

Of course, some body parts are more prolific than others. Head and shoulders above the rest is *head* (from Old English *heafod*, "top of the body"), which has given us *headline*, *head of a golf club*, *headquarters*, *headstrong*, *headway*, *headrest*, and *heads-up*.

"Very interesting," you say (I hope). "But where's the connection to *cabbage* and *captain*?"

What we have here is an example of rival words. When the Normans brought French to England, they brought a great many "head" words based on the Latin *caput*. These included *cap*, *captain* ("head person"), *capital*, and *capitulation*, which refers to the "headlines" in a document containing the conditions of surrender.

And *cabbage*? It comes to our table from the Middle French *caboche*, "head."

calcium & calculus

When little kids work out sums on their fingers, their efforts seem unconnected to the world of abstract mathematics. And yet, as etymology shows us, calculus itself is rooted in something just as tangible as finger counting.

Calcium comes from the Latin *calx*, "limestone," a building material derived from the remains of mollusks and other sea animals. Calcium, of course, is a key element in the formation of bones, without which children couldn't count on their fingers.

But the relationship with mathematics is more roundabout than that. The word *calculus* entered English directly from an identically spelled Latin word meaning "to reckon." Originally, the Latin word referred to a pebble used for counting. Those pebbles were often made of limestone, which explains why *calculus* itself derived from *calx*.

The notion of counting tangible things as the foundation for mathematics is revealed also in the word *digital*, from the Latin *digitus*, meaning "finger" or "toe"—which came to mean a number presented by any one of those body parts. It doesn't take all that much imagination to see switches inside a modern computer as electronic representations of fingers and toes.

Which brings us back to young children learning to calculate by putting one group of fingers next to another group and then counting the result.

Next stop: MIT.

calcium & *calculus*

canary & canine

Zoologists have discovered amazing similarities between animals that at first glance seem to have little in common. For example, despite their huge difference in size, mice and giraffes have the exact same number of neck bones. But to figure out the link between *canary* and *canine*, you need an etymologist as much as a biologist.

Canine comes from the Latin *canis*, "dog." The same Latin word gave rise to *kennel* and to *chenille*, a velvety—some would say hairy—yarn or fabric.

Canis is found unchanged in "Canis Major," the name of a constellation containing Sirius, the Dog Star, which is the brightest star seen from Earth. Actually Sirius is a binary star, meaning that it's two stars that are close enough that they appear to be one.

Sirius has an interesting biography, but we haven't space to go into it here. Instead, we must return to Earth, specifically to an island located off the northwest coast of Africa. Here, Roman explorers met up with bands of large, fierce dogs and used the Latin term *canine* to name the island—Gran Canaria. That island and others nearby came to be known as the Canary Islands.

On the Canary Islands explorers discovered colorful songbirds belonging to the finch family. Ultimately these birds were named "canaries" for the islands that had been named for the dogs that shared the territory.

canary & canine

candid & candidate

Many of us who were introduced to the word *candid* by the television show "Candid Camera" first believed that the term meant "secret" or "sneaky." This is not surprising given the fact that the program used a hidden camera to capture people in a variety of hilarious situations.

But eventually we learned that the true meaning of *candid* was almost the opposite. Along with its close relative *candle*, *candid* traces back to the Latin *candere*, "to shine." By the seventeenth century metaphorical extension had given *candid* the contemporary meaning of "being honest or frank in what one says."

A cynic might wonder: "But what does candor (to use another offshoot of *candere*) have to do with *candidate?*" To answer that question, we must return to ancient Rome. There, we find the Latin word *candidatus* naming the shining white togas worn by Roman office seekers. *Candidatus*, of course, comes from *candere*.

This etymology leads us to speculate that Thomas Jefferson—who wrote, "The whole of government consists in the art of being honest"—would rather watch "Candid Camera" than coverage of contemporary election campaigns with their incendiary rhetoric that sheds more heat than light.

Or as the homey philosopher Kin Hubbard put it, "We'd all like to vote for the best man, but he's never a candidate."

cartoon & Magna Carta

Samuel Goldwyn was alleged to have said, "An oral contract isn't worth the paper it's written on." That witticism, whoever actually first said it, pays backhanded homage to the importance of getting things down on paper.

The Magna Carta, issued in 1215, is a good example. From the Latin *magna*, "great," and *carta*, "paper," it specifically limited the power of the English crown, but—of more lasting importance— was the first step in the journey that led to the rule of law and guarantees of personal freedom, including the freedom of expression.

Which brings us to *cartoon*, first used in 1843 by the publisher of the British magazine *Punch* as the name of a satiric drawing, often accompanied by a few words. *Cartoon* was borrowed from the French *carton*, "pasteboard," which artists used in the seventeenth century for making sketches, particularly for frescoes. *Carton*, used today to name a box made of thick paper, traces back to the Latin *carta*, met above, from which we also get *chart*, *cartography*, *a la carte*, *carte blanche*, and *cartridge*, originally a charge of gunpowder rolled in strong paper.

Although *Punch* gave the cartoon its name, the magazine didn't originate the genre. Revolutionary-era artists on both sides of the Atlantic created cartoons mocking each other, often viciously. By the time of the American Civil War, the venomous style of cartooning had become a tradition. Many of the political cartoons about Lincoln were labeled by his supporters as racist and obscene.

The more things change . . .

champagne & champion

When you see the victors in a sports competition spraying each other with bubbly, you may think that they're being childish. But in reality—or at least in the reality of etymology—the zany celebration makes perfect sense, for it dramatizes the connection between *champagne* and *champion*.

Although sparkling wine can be produced from grapes grown in many places around the world, traditionally only wine made with grapes grown in the French jurisdiction of Champagne-Ardenne may be called "Champagne." The beverage Champagne was invented around 1700. But the word's origins extend back much farther. Until the thirteenth century, Champagne, the place, was an independent entity. A region of forests and lakes, it took its name from the Latin *campania*, "level country," which itself is derived from the Latin *campus*, "a field." This is, of course, the source of the kind of *campus* that houses a university or, in more recent usage, an organization developing products.

While the fields of Champagne were perfect for growing grapes, other fields in ancient times were better suited for warfare, and that brings us to *champion*, a valiant fighter or—more usually—the victor in a contest to determine the best among all other competitors. Around the time that Champagne was becoming part of France, English borrowed the word *champion* from the Old French *champion*, which came from the Latin *campio*, "warrior in the field," which in turn came from the Latin *campus*, literally "field" but in this context "field of combat."

Thus in a championship Champagne shower, we have the victor in one kind of field being anointed with wine grown in another kind of field—much more fitting than to douse such a champion with coffee, tea, or milk.

champagne & champion

chaos *&* gasoline

The 1973 gasoline crisis, which created chaos in the United States and around the world, took most people by surprise. But a little etymological knowledge might have served as a heads-up then . . . and it still might today.

The term *gasoline* was coined in 1865. For the moment, let's skip the first syllable and consider the letters *ol*, derived from *oleum*—Latin for "olive oil." *Oleum*, which traces back to the Greek *elaion*, "olive tree," is also found in the word *petroleum*, the term for *gasoline* used in most places outside of North America. A slightly different form of *oleum* appears in *oleomargarine*.

The *-ine* in *gasoline* is a suffix used in naming chemicals and in forming commercial product names, such as Vaseline.

Now let's deal with *gasoline*'s initial syllable *gas*. In the 1600s, the Flemish chemist Jan Baptist van Helmont, who helped establish modern scientific techniques, used *gas* to name the volatile substances produced during his chemical experiments. He either derived the word from the Greek *khaos*, "empty space," or he borrowed it from the earlier writings of the alchemist Paracelsus. Either way, if we study the word's origin, we can discover the word's hidden warning.

For the Greeks *khaos* meant "chasm" or "void." The word was used biblically to suggest the absolute nothingness that existed before the creation of the universe. Anyone contemplating the cosmological abyss can perhaps understand why *chaos* eventually came to mean "extreme confusion."

We are cautioned not to breathe in the fumes as we gas up our car. Perhaps the etymology of *gas* may serve as an additional warning that if we rely too much on the system that brings the gas to the pump, we might drive ourselves directly into chaos.

circuit *&* circus

An *aptronym* is a name that links to the name owner's work—for example, "James Bugg," an exterminator. Closer to the topic at hand is the name Ringling, belonging to the siblings who created a celebrated three-*ring* circus.

Although we associate the circus with clowns, acrobats, animals, and animal trainers, the word *circus* refers not to the talent but to the stage. *Circus* comes from the Greek *kirkos*, "a circle," as in the famous London roundabout Piccadilly Circus. The Greeks and later the Romans mounted their entertainments within circular arenas, which ultimately became the Ringling brothers' rings.

Etymologists have traced *circus*, and its close relative *circle*, back to a hypothetical European word meaning "to turn," the operation that would generate a circle, a figure whose beginning and ending are one and the same.

The ancients were particularly fond of the circle, believing it to be a natural and perfect figure. Thus, Aristotle maintained that planetary orbits had to be circular. For centuries this idea held back advances in astronomy until Johannes Kepler had the wit and courage to suggest that the orbits were actually elliptical.

Kepler's eccentric thinking perhaps made it possible for *kirkos*-spawned words to refer to noncircular realities. A good example is *circuit*, which names the path along which a current flows. Traveling workers of every sort—including judges, preachers, and vaudevillians—used the same word to refer to their noncircular journeys. The concept is found in many words and phrases, such as *circulatory system*, *circumnavigate*, and *circumlocution*. Which brings us back to the traveling circus making its yearly circuit.

companion & pantry

If you like bread, you probably agree with the Chinese proverb: "When you have only two pennies left in the world, buy a loaf of bread with one and a lily with the other." As a bread lover, you're probably also interested in memorable facts, such as:

- Marie Antoinette never said, "If they can't find bread, let them eat cake."
- The croissant was invented in Austria to commemorate a victory over the Turks.
- The French buy baguettes at least once a day because French bread is fat-free and hence gets stale within hours.

But what has this to do with *companion* and *pantry*? Let's see.

Companion goes back to the Latin *companio*, made up of *com*, "with," plus *panis*, "bread," literally "with bread"—and implicitly someone you'd gladly break bread with. The same Latin word gave us *company*, which refers either to a group of soldiers or to a business organization.

The Latin *panis* is the source of the modern French word for bread, *pain*. *Panis* also gave rise to an Old French word, *paneterie*, "bread room," the place where ingredients and tools were stored for making bread and other foods. When it was imported into English, *paneterie* became *pantry*.

The French word *pain*, however, was no match for the well-established Middle English word *bred*, referring to the same thing. Soon, for English speakers, the *pan* in *pantry* had no association to "bread," which may explain why many people could think that *pantry* is etymologically related to *pan*. But etymological companions, such as you and I, will never make that mistake.

competition & petition

The Bill of Rights guarantees to the people the right "to petition the Government for a redress of grievances." But exactly what does *petition* mean, and how does it relate to that key ingredient of the American way of life: *competition*?

Petition, originally meaning "a prayer," came into English from the Latin *petitio*, "a request," which itself derived from *petere*, a verb with two personalities, one nonviolent—"to seek"—and the other aggressive—"to attack." We get the idea that if "nice" doesn't work, there is a plan B. Sort of like "good cop, bad cop." In other words, to petition isn't a wimpy sort of gesture, but an action that means business. This isn't surprising given what we know about the revolutionaries who launched the country. The founding fathers believed that the right to petition would help keep the government in check.

Competition relates exclusively to the aggressive side of *petition*. Entering English from the French *competer*, "to rival," it traces back to the Latin compound *competere* made up of *com-*, "together," and *petere*, "to seek." The sense of the word is of rivals seeking the same goal within a framework of laws and rules. The competitors have, in a real way, come together for the purpose of testing each other. As Henry John Kaiser put it: "Live daringly, boldly, fearlessly. Taste the relish to be found in competition—in having put forth the best within you."

complex & complexion

Domestic activities such as planting and spinning were used metaphorically to generate many words. A good example is *complex*, as in Oedipus complex. The word *complex* comes to us from the Latin adjective *complexus*—"woven." Something complex consists of two or more elements that are intricately woven together in a way that challenges comprehension. Freud, for example, employed lengthy dream interpretations to help his patients unravel their complexes.

At first glance, *complexion* would seem to be the opposite of all this, something that is on the surface and immediately perceivable. The solution to this etymological mystery is that in the fourteenth century *complexion* referred to the combination of the four humors—blood, phlegm, choler, and melancholy—believed by medieval physicians to determine a patient's health and temperament. Eventually, the word was extended to refer to the overall impression given by the color and texture of a person's facial skin.

Of course, if you don't like your complexion, that could give rise to an inferiority complex, which you might deal with in analysis, or perhaps by applying a bit of makeup. Your choice.

computer & reputation

Artists have long explored the meaning of reputation. In *Othello*, Shakespeare gives Iago these memorable lines:

> *Good name in man and woman, dear my lord is the*
> *immediate jewel of their souls:*
> *Who steals my purse steals trash; 'tis something, nothing;*
> *But he that filches from me my good name*
> *Robs me of that which not enriches him*
> *And makes me poor indeed.*

Stanley Kubrick's *2001: A Space Odyssey* goes a step further by including machines among those concerned with reputation. When Dr. Dave Bowman, an astronaut, questions the infallibility of HAL 9000, the ship's smooth-talking robot, HAL replies petulantly: "Dave, I don't know how else to put this, but it just happens to be an unalterable fact that I am incapable of being wrong."

But *doing* wrong is another matter, and HAL goes on a murderous rampage. It's deliciously apt that the tarnishing of his reputation is what pushes the computer over the edge, for both *reputation* and *computer* trace back to the Latin *putare*, "to reckon," a word that encompasses solving mathematical and moral problems, implied in the phrase "day of reckoning."

In the mid-seventeenth century, *computer* referred to a person who knew how to compute, for example, a bookkeeper in a shop. The human computer was far from error-free, and Kubrick dramatizes the fact that machine computers are bound to inherit the weaknesses of the human computers that built them.

coronation & coroner

Coronation brings to mind an event that is rare and glamorous—the stuff of fairytales—whereas *coroner* suggests a happening that is routine, and bloody—the stuff of American TV cop shows. How in the world do these two words flock together?

Coronation comes from the Latin *coronare*, "to crown," which traces back to *corona*, "crown." Go one more step back and you come to the Greek *korone*, "a curved object, a wreath."

No surprises here, nor with the metaphorical extension of *corona* as the name for the ring of fire seen around the sun during a solar eclipse. Likewise if we saw an anatomical picture of the arteries arrayed around the heart, we could understand why those blood vessels are called the *coronary arteries*.

But coroner? Where's the glitter in determining what killed someone? This time, a picture won't help us. We need the etymologist's research, which in this case tells us that originally a coroner was an official charged with caring for the royal property, which naturally included crowns. Gradually following the rise of civil government after the granting of the Magna Carta, the coroner was assigned other, less noble duties, but ones that some might argue are far more important or at least—in television murder shows—more dramatic.

cosmetics & cosmos

"If I have been able to see farther than others," said Isaac Newton, "it is because I stood on the shoulders of giants."

One of those giants was Pythagoras, the Greek mathematician, who might have been the first to use *kosmos* ("order") as the name for the universe. This was nearly three millenniums before modern scientists started playing with the concepts of the Big Bang and chaos.

Whether or not the universe is actually well ordered, to the ancients orderliness was at the heart of beauty. *Kosmos* had spun off *kosmetikos*, "skilled in adornment," a word that entered English as *cosmetics* shortly before Newton developed his theories about orderly forces that held the cosmos together.

The use of cosmetics is more ancient than the word, as demonstrated by Egyptian art dating from 4000 B.C. And controversies about cosmetics are also old news. In the eighteenth century, European governments considered enacting a law that would criminalize using cosmetics for the purpose of seduction.

crisis & criticism

As with people, some words have undeservedly bad reputations. The pair of words here is a classic example. Perhaps with the help of etymology, we can improve their status.

Words typically given as synonyms for *crisis* include *disaster* ("great and sudden misfortune"), *catastrophe* ("bringing overthrow or ruin"), and *calamity* ("deep trouble, misery"). No wonder that many people lose hope when crises occur, whether at the personal level (such as during a midlife crisis) or on the international front. The good news is that optimism can be found at the etymological root of *crisis*. The word comes from the Greek *krisis*, "turning point," which goes back to the verb *krinein*, "to discriminate, to weigh, to decide."

John Kennedy (or one of his speechwriters) caught the true sense of the word in the following: "The Chinese use two brush strokes to write the word *crisis*. One brush stroke stands for danger; the other for opportunity. In a crisis, be aware of the danger—but recognize the opportunity."

As with *crisis*, synonyms for *criticism* are often negative, for example, *faultfinding* and *disapproval*. Yet the origins of *criticism* trace back to the same Greek root as *crisis*: *krinein*. In this context the meaning is "to analyze for the purpose of improving."

It's true, as Franklin Jones wrote, that "honest criticism is hard to take, particularly from a relative, a friend, an acquaintance, or a stranger." But in the words of Elbert Hubbard the only way to avoid criticism is to "do nothing, say nothing, be nothing."

If criticism has a bad rap, it is perhaps because too many professional critics can't resist the fun of putting someone down. But, of course, I'm not speaking of anyone reviewing this book.

cult & culture

Cult has a thoroughly negative connotation, suggesting something secret and evil. Yet it shares parentage with *culture*, one of the most positive words in English, a word suggesting tradition, refinement, and civilization itself.

Etymologically, *cult* and *culture* are almost twins. Both derive from the Latin *cultura*, meaning "to till." In an era when most people worked the land, farming generated many positive symbols and images. The kindness of the gods was demonstrated by bountiful harvests.

Over the centuries, *culture* took on metaphorical meanings such as refinement through education. Later it was used to name the intellectual and artistic achievements of a society.

Meanwhile, in the seventeenth century, *cult* was coined as a word describing a nontraditional form of worship. By the nineteenth century, its focus was on primitive rituals.

Then, in the mid-twentieth century *cult* came to label recently developed groups that mainstream organizations considered out of step and counterculture. The word was used pejoratively to marginalize such groups. Interestingly, researchers discovered two facts about cults: First, members of modern cults rarely use the term *cult* to refer to themselves except for humorous effect (I belong to the "Cult of Bad-Movie Lovers"). Second, characteristics identified as "cultish"—for example, the vow of poverty—are as likely to be found in established organizations as they are in cults. The only provable differences are that cults are recently formed and also that they have fewer members.

dandelion & dentist

When they were growing up, future dentists—like most kids—probably puffed the seeds of the dandelion plant and made a wish or did some other folk incantation. That playful activity gives us a tiny hint about the etymological link between these two words.

The origin of *dentist* is fairly straightforward. The word comes to English via the French *dent*, "tooth," which came from the Latin *dens*, "tooth." You can glimpse variations of the Latin root in words such as *denture* and *orthodontist*.

Indentation is a metaphorical extension; originally it referred to notches cut into paired copies of a contract; matching up the tooth-like cuts showed that each copy was authentic. Later, the word was applied to the typographic notches indicating the start of paragraphs—for example, the indentation of the word *indentation* beginning the paragraph you are reading right now.

The same sort of metaphorical thinking led to naming the familiar dandelion weed. But there is a twist. The English word is a borrowing of the French *dent-de-lion*, literally "tooth of the lion" or "lion's tooth." To some folk botanist, the leaves of this ubiquitous plant resembled the sharp teeth of the king of beasts.

As often happens when one language borrows a word from another language, the borrowers can't say the word as it's pronounced in the original language. Instead, they assimilate the foreign sounds to familiar sounds. So the elements *dent-de*, which in French sound something like "dawn-day" (pardon my French) came out sounding more like "dandy." After all, dandelions do make dandy playthings.

dandelion & dentist

deadline & linen

People who write about writing favor words like *imagery* and *inspiration*. But for the working stiff—the journalist, the professional novelist, the ad writer—*deadline* comes more often to mind.

Deadline is obviously compounded from *dead* and *line*. *Dead* is one of those sturdy, four-letter Old English words that seemingly have been in the language forever—not traceable to Latin or Greek. Surprisingly, the homely word *line* has a more interesting biography. Although it too is an Old English word, it can be traced back further to the Latin phrase *linea restis*, from *linea*, "linen," and *restis*, "string."

Eventually, *line* was clipped from *linea restis*, and, presumably because a piece of thread could be pulled straight, it came to name the geometric figure that joins any two points. Linen, of course, was also used to make cloth, which in ancient times was used to wrap the dead. But we're more interested in the fact that *line* semantically flowered to give us a plethora of words, including: *linear*, *lineage*, ocean *liner*, a *line* of poetry, *pipeline*, *streamline*, and newspaper *headline*, which—even though a line is supposed to be straight—brings us back to *deadline*.

We may wonder why a simple cut-off date deserves such a scary synonym as *deadline*. Perhaps the word was coined when editors threatened procrastinating writers with death if they didn't get the copy in on time. Or maybe, as etymologist Douglas Harper suggests, it's a borrowing from Civil War prisons where *dead-line* referred to a physical boundary "over which no man could pass and live."

decide & scissors

If you have trouble making decisions, your neighborhood linguist might suggest that you think of yourself as a pair of scissors.

Here's the logic behind this etymological advice. *Scissors* comes to us from the Latin *cædere*, "to cut." Similarly, *decide* traces back to the Latin *decædere*. The prefix *de-* means "off." Thus *decædere* means "to cut off." When you're faced with a decision, for example, whether to become a doctor or a writer, you must metaphorically cut apart the two possibilities. You'll keep one and discard the other.

In case you worry that you might have made the wrong choice, consider the following:

> "Once a decision was made, I did not worry about it afterward."
>
> —HARRY TRUMAN

> "Ever notice that 'what the hell' is always the right decision?"
>
> —MARILYN MONROE

(Note: I prefer using only one quote per essay, but I just couldn't decide which one you'd like better. Probably I have no future as a decision maker, or even as a pair of scissors.)

---

decimal & decimate

Decimate is a classic example of "semantic inflation." Just like people, words can exaggerate.

The story begins with the Latin prefix *deci-*, "ten." *Deci-* and its Greek relative *deka* spawned a variety of words such as *decade*, *Decalogue* (the Ten Commandments), and *decimal*, a fraction with an implied denominator of ten. All cut and dried meanings.

Decimate comes from the Latin *decem*, "ten," and *-atus*, a suffix denoting an action, hence "taking of one-tenth." The Romans used the word in two ways. First, it referred to imposing a tax of 10 percent, comparable to the meaning of the English word *tithe*. Second, it referred to the Roman army's method of punishing an offending group—citizens or soldiers—by killing one in ten via a lottery. This too was a very specific operation.

However, as the word began to be applied to loss of life from other causes, such as fires, floods, famine, and plagues, it came to mean not merely a loss of one tenth, but something closer to annihilation.

denouement & noose

Noose sounds like the sort of word that grew up in the Old West, a dusty term suited to frontier justice.

Denouement, on the other hand, has a wonderfully sophisticated feel about it, especially if—like the French—you pronounce the final syllable nasally. If you're not confident about your pronunciation, try pinching your nose shut as you say the word while imagining yourself chatting with the literati at the Algonquin Hotel, circa 1920.

Yet strange as it seems, the two words are closely related. *Noose* comes not from the American West but from the south of France. It derives from Old Provincial *nous*, "knot," which traces back to the Latin *nodus*, "knot."

Denouement comes from the same knotty root by way of the Old French *desnouer*, "to untie." In other words, *denouement* is the place in the story where the plot is unraveled.

The word is in the long tradition of fiber-based literary expressions. The most memorable example is *clue*, from the Old English *cleowen*, "ball of yarn," an allusion to the story of Theseus, a Greek hero who escaped from the Labyrinth by following a long thread. The same idea is contained in the nineteenth-century sailors' phrase "spinning a yarn."

The complex etymology you just read may itself seem like a yarn. But why shouldn't truth be stranger than fiction? "Fiction, after all," explained Mark Twain, "has to make sense."

derive&rival

Attempting to discover the original form of a word—its ety-mon—is like tracing a stream to its source. Sometimes rival etymologists identify different etymons for the same word, leading to wars of words. All of which will make more sense when we take a closer look at the two words above.

Derive comes to us from the Latin *de-*, "from," and *rivus*, "stream." Originally, it meant leading a stream from its regular path, perhaps to irrigate a field. Around Shakespeare's time it acquired the metaphorical meaning of "deducing" or "inferring," as "inferring the origin of a word."

Rival comes from the Latin *rivalis*, meaning a person who uses the same stream as another person or a person on the other side of the stream, hence, a competitor for the benefits of the stream, for example, fish or water.

Around the time that *derive* took on its modern meaning, *rival*—again via metaphorical extension—came to mean any competitor, for example, a linguist proposing a competing etymon.

dictator & dictionary

Dictator and *dictionary* bring to mind very different images—the former, a brutal tyrant using guns and tanks to control the masses; the latter, diligent students flipping Webster's pages in order to build their vocabularies and refine their minds.

But in fact, the two words are closely related etymologically. *Dictator* traces back to the Latin verb *dicere*, "to say." The first dictators were Roman judges who—under extraordinary conditions perhaps analogous to the modern-day imposition of martial law—were given absolute power. Their word was law.

Dicere is the source of a huge number of English words including *dictate*, *dictum*, *contradict*, *verdict*, *edict*, *indict*, *predict*, and—for you grammar enthusiasts—*diction* and *predicate*.

Dictionary, of course, belongs in this list, being the depository of the raw materials needed to say something. The name comes from the Latin *dictionarius*, "of words." Although *dictionarius* is a thirteenth-century coinage, dictionary making dates back at least two thousand years.

Dictator and *dictionary* are also related in reality—not that etymology isn't real. At the time Adolf Hitler was winning the hearts and minds of the German people with his masterfully manipulative speeches, Herbert Hoover wrote, "Every dictator has climbed to power on the ladder of free speech. Immediately on attaining power each dictator has suppressed all free speech except his own."

divulge & vulgar

I want to divulge something but not to everyone. If you view yourself as upper crust, please skip ahead to the next entry. This one is for the rest of us: the unwashed masses, the ordinary folks, the "wretched refuse" mentioned on the Statue of Liberty, all who are looked down on as *vulgar*.

(Are *we the people* alone? Okay.)

Here's some good news: vulgar isn't bad, although the elite might like us to believe so. The dictionary defines *vulgar* as characteristic of the masses—their foolish beliefs, their unrefined speech, their popular culture. Synonyms for *vulgar* include *coarse*, *crude*, *boorish*, *indecent*, *obscene*. As you can guess, dictionaries are not written by the "little guy," which is too bad because there is another, more positive side to the word.

Vulgar comes from the Latin *vulgus*, "the common people." These are the folks who created Vulgar Latin, the everyday speech of Rome, which gave rise to the Romance languages: Italian, Spanish, and French. Vulgar Latin was also the language that St. Jerome used in the fourth century to write the Vulgate Bible, which for centuries was read in the Roman Catholic Church.

In divulging these facts about the true facts about *vulgar*, I am not simply revealing secrets but rather democratizing important information as the etymology of *divulge* makes clear. *Divulge* comes from the Latin *divulgare*, "to spread among the common people." We the Vulgar might choose as our hero William Gladstone, who rhymed: "All the world over, I will back the masses against the classes."

Amen, brother.

doctor & indoctrinate

Doctors are easy to make fun of. A quick look into the history books reveals many practices—such as bleeding George Washington to death—of questionable value.

In his *Devil's Dictionary*, Ambrose Bierce summed up our ambivalence to doctors like this:

> Physician, n. One upon whom we set our hopes when ill and our dogs when well.

And yet, for all the jokes, doctors continue to be held in high esteem. From our own experiences and from the many television programs that dramatize medicine, we get the picture of doctors as masters of observing, analyzing, assessing, prescribing, and comforting.

Sometimes they also try to indoctrinate us regarding habits that might lead away from illness and toward wellness. Although this effort may seem unscientific, and sometimes isn't welcomed, it makes perfect sense—at least from the etymological point of view. *Indoctrinate* comes from the Latin *in-* plus *docere*, "to teach." *Doctor* traces back to the exact same root.

Moral: The next time your physician suggests that you eat less or walk more or quit worrying, be glad—as the proverb councils—that you don't live in a town where there are no doctors.

dribble & droopy

Sports fans, this one's for you. But if you're guessing it's just about basketball, you can drop that idea. However, don't drop *drop*, because it's a big part of the story.

For starters, *dribble* didn't start with basketball. It was first a soccer expression dating from the 1830s and referring to a series of short kicks. Basketball was invented by James Naismith slightly more than half a century later. The rules prohibited running with the ball (a violation now known as "traveling"), but players could advance the ball—originally, a soccer ball—by batting at it.

This somehow brought to mind the soccer term *dribbling*, based on a sixteenth-century word *drib* (as in "dribs and drabs"), which was a variant of *drip*. *Drip* came into Middle English from the Middle Danish *drippe*. Or perhaps it came from the Old English *dropian*, "to drop," sort of what happens when you dribble a basketball.

You don't need an etymologist to make the connection between *droop* and *drop*. Just think of what happens to your shoulders when you droop them. But for those who demand proof, *droop* comes from the Old Norse *drupa*, "to drop," a close relative of the Old English *dropian*.

dubious & duplicitous

Although etymologists rely on texts to uncover the origins of words, sometimes a bit of introspection can help. Here's a case in point.

When you're dubious about a course of action, what's going on inside you? To make this more concrete, imagine that someone lays out a business proposal. The person says: "You invest $10,000 in my motion picture project. If it's a hit, you'll earn $100,000." And you think: "It could be a hit, but it could be a bust."

That sense of seeing two possible outcomes goes to the heart of being dubious, which word comes to us from the Latin *dubius*, "doubt." *Dubius* itself traces back to *duo*, "two." The concept is: when you're in doubt, you are not sure which of two possibilities will in fact be the outcome.

It's roughly the same story with *duplicitous*, which traces to the Latin *duplicitas*, "doubleness." In other words, someone who is duplicitous acts in two ways, for example, as an ally and as an enemy. The closely related Latin *duplicatus*, from which we get the modern *duplicate*, derives from an older but related word, *duo*, "two." The modern word *duo*, "pair," entered English from Italian, along with its companion *duet*.

economy & nemesis

For many politicians—and plain folks, too—the economy proves to be their nemesis. Is it fate or is it etymology?

Economy comes from the Greek *oikonomia*, "household management," a compound made up of *oikos*, "house," and *nomos*, "manage." The element *nomos* traces back to the verb *nemein*, literally "to distribute." It was this meaning that generated the word *nomadic*, referring to wandering herders who would divide up the pasturelands that they came upon. Applied more generally, *nomos* gave rise to *economy*, any system for distributing the goods. Nothing in the term suggests a fair distribution. That's a topic for a more controversial book.

What interests us here is the connection with *nemesis*. The word originated with *Nemesis*, the Greek goddess of vengeance, who played a part—often offstage—in many Greek literary works. Nemesis, whose name derives from *nemein*, which we learned above means "to distribute," made sure that people "got what they deserved." Given the nature of people—to err being human—these just deserts often took the form of serious punishment. Which insight led to the contemporary definition of *nemesis* as any force that brings someone down.

Returning to our politicians: If they mismanage the economy, it is pure justice that they meet their nemesis.

erudite *&* rude

If you want to be considered *erudite*, the most important fact you need to know is how to pronounce the word: "AIR you dite." Go ahead, try it. You'll be way ahead of unerudite folks who unfortunately say "AIR oo dite," which is the old-fashioned way of saying the word.

Just in case anyone asks you, *erudite* comes from the Latin *eruditus*, a word formed from *e-* (shortened from *ex-*), "out," plus *rudis*, "unskilled, rough." In other words, an erudite person has come out of roughness. *Education* has a parallel etymology: *e-* plus *ducare*, "to lead." Hence, a teacher leads students out of ignorance.

Like *erudite*, *rude* traces back to *rudis* and originally referred to rough surfaces of wood and other materials. We see this usage in the first lines of Ralph Waldo Emerson's "Concord Hymn" about the opening battle of the American Revolution:

> By the rude bridge that arched the flood,
> Their flag to April's breeze unfurled;
> Here once the embattled farmers stood;
> And fired the shot heard round the world.

Through metaphoric extension, *rude* eventually was applied to people who were not yet "finished" or "polished." Can we call them "diamonds in the rough"? It was only later—via a process called *semantic deterioration*—that *rude* acquired such negative meanings as "impolite," "uncouth," "foul," and "offensive."

excrement & secret

"Three may keep a secret," wrote Ben Franklin, "if two of them are dead." Ben's sardonic witticism suggests the etymology of *secret*.

Secret traces back to the Latin adjective *secretus*, a compound made up of *se*, "apart," and *cretus*, "separated." This gives us the literal meaning of "set apart." Hence, a *secret* is knowledge kept apart—kept separate—from others. An exception, of course, would be one's *secretary*, a person entrusted with secrets—sometimes a misplaced trust as certain members of the British royalty can attest to.

But what has this to do with *excrement*? Here's the poop: The letters *cre*, which we see also in *secret*, give us a clue. *Excrement* goes back to the Latin *excretus*. The first syllable *ex-* (as in *exit*) means "out," and *cretus*, as we learned above, means "separated." Literally, *excrement* refers to "separated out," in other words, "discharged."

Shhhhhh.

execute & sequel

Leaving ethicists to debate the pros and cons of capital punishment, word purists often grumble about the phrase "execute the prisoner," which treats *execute* as a synonym for "kill." Whether the killing is done by rope, lethal injection, electricity, or any other method, those who know the true history of *execute* proclaim that the word is getting a bad rap. Let's dispassionately look at the evidence.

Execute derives from the Latin word *sequi*, "to follow." The same Latin word gave rise to *sequel*, which is a story that follows an earlier story, usually featuring many of the same characters and even continuing the plot line. But if you've seen *Star Trek 87*, you already know this.

So what does "following" have to do with "killing"? Hold on, we're almost there. But first we need to look at *executive*, which obviously relates to *execute*. An executive is someone who follows—carries out—the wishes of another person or organization. For example, as chief executive of the United States, the president executes—follows—the laws of Congress.

Similarly, an executioner is hired to execute the court's instructions to kill the prisoner. It is the court's *order* that is executed, not the prisoner. The prisoner is done away with only because the order is executed—in other words, "followed."

But here's a warning to any English teacher or word lover who hopes to win the linguistic battle to ban the expression "the prisoner was executed." That "illogical" usage of "executing a prisoner" was already well established by the fifteenth century!

fable & fib

The connection between *fable* and *fabulous* is obvious, both words deriving from an ancient Latin word *fabula*, "story." *Fab* as in the Fab Four (the Beatles) is clipped from *fabulous*.

(We interrupt this etymology to present an important message to authors hoping to write for the ages: Beware of overblown, over-used advertising words like *fabulous*. You don't want your texts littered with obsolete slang such as *boffo*, *ripping*, and *smashing*.)

Back to the matter of linking *fib* with *fable*. Meaning a small, innocuous lie—if there is such a thing—*fib* comes from *fible-fable*, a now-extinct reduplication meaning "nonsense."

Ah, but you ask, "What is a reduplication?" It's a word made by the playful process of repeating a syllable often with the change of a single letter. Other examples include *mumbo-jumbo*, *walkie-talkie*, *chit-chat*, *palsy-walsy* and—for those of you into nostalgia—a dance called the Hokey Pokey.

In *fible-fable*, it's fable that contributes the sense of untruth, with *fible* adding the fun.

flamboyant & in flagrante delicto

If you want to call attention to yourself, go for red—red shoes, red car, red hair—or if you're a flamingo, red feathers. This is the lesson taught by *flamboyant*, a word first used in the fifteenth century to name a showy—flaming—style of French architecture. The word traces back to the Old French *flamboyer*, "flame," and further to the Latin *flagare*, "to burn."

From the same Latin source we get many hot English words. These include *flambe, inflammatory, inflammation, flagrant*, and—coming to the point of this entry—*in flagrante delicto*. A literal translation of this Latin legal expression is "with the crime still blazing." Figuratively, we get "in the act of committing the crime" or "red-handed."

These days, of course, *in flagrante delicto* almost always refers to the "crime" of an illicit sexual encounter. Hot stuff. Which brings to mind a seventeenth-century synonym for "sweetheart"—*flame*.

flatulence &inflation

Flatulence and *inflation* represent events that most people dislike, the exceptions being kids who find flatulence (or at least the sound of it) amusing and investors in gold who find inflation lucrative.

Despite the fact that they come from the same root, the two words have opposite meanings—one describing an outward flow, the other an inward flow.

Flatulence comes from the Latin *flare*, literally "to blow," figuratively "to break wind." By the end of the sixteenth century, *flatulence* had become a euphemism for the Old English *fart*, not one of the famous "seven dirty words" banned from U.S. broadcast media, but still generally taboo. Although Microsoft Word fails to recognize the word in its thesaurus, *fart* is widely used by the masses and has close relatives in German (*farzen*), Swedish (*fjarta*), and Danish (*fjerte*).

Inflation is a sixteenth-century word derived from the Latin compound *inflare*, from the prefix *in-*, "in," + *flare*, "blow," literally "blow into." Originally, *inflation* meant blowing up balloons. By the 1830s, the word was used metaphorically to describe the expansion of the money supply.

I'll bet you a gazillion dollars *inflation* will remain in use at least as long as *flatulence*.

flimflam & flimsy

Flimflam, which means both "nonsense" and "a sneaky trick," is an example of reduplication. As noted in the fable entry, reduplication is a playful word-making process in which one element—the base—is repeated in a slightly altered and usually meaningless form. Sometimes reduplication results in a rhyme: *hurly-burly*, *Humpty-Dumpty*, and *Fuzzy Wuzzy*.

Although the origin of *flimflam* is uncertain, some etymologists tentatively identify *flam* as the base word, which they trace to the old English *flamfew*, "a trifle."

The author of this book humbly suggests an alternative: that the base is *flim*, clipped from *flimsy*, "something poorly made."

Unfortunately, the evidence for this idea is . . . flimsy. And the fact that current research dates *flimflam* from 1538 and *flimsy* from 1702 doesn't help. But etymology dating is often a work in progress because it rests on discovering a word in a text. Thus, it is possible that *flimsy* is much older than *flimflam*.

What we need is to find *flimflam* in a piece of literature—a diary, a poem, a story, a letter, an e-mail—from before 1538, preferably written in Old English or Middle English.

Otherwise, some skeptical fuddy-duddy may view this entry as an example of flimflam or mumbo jumbo or even funky junky.

fornicate & furnace

Almost every book on etymology deals with the "F" word. Why should *Words of a Feather* be an exception?

Around the time that Saint Augustine wrote, "Lord give me chastity, but not yet," Roman architecture was celebrated for its arches. And that brings us to *fornication*, from the Latin *fornicari*, "fornicate." *Fornicari* comes from the Latin *fornix*, figuratively "brothel," but literally "arch" or "vaulted chamber." *Fornix* goes back further to *fornus*, "an oven designed with an arched top" and the source of *furnace*.

What does all this heat have to do with sex? This is where it gets interesting, at least from an etymological point of view. According to those who keep track of such matters, prostitutes in ancient Rome waited for their Giovannis (johns) while standing under arches or near the arch-shaped ovens that baked the bread Romans widely enjoyed.

Given the heat from the ovens, and the metaphorical heat of sensual encounters (think about a dog being in heat), we can easily imagine the connection between *fornicate* and *furnace*. At least some of us can imagine it.

gladiator & gladiolus

Whether you're into violent sports or into backyard gardening—or both—this entry will probably interest you. It's got pomp, circumstance, swords, athletes of both sexes, and a full rainbow of colors.

The action begins in ancient Roman arenas where gladiators fought each other and wild animals, often to the death. *Gladiator*, "swordsman," comes from *gladius*, a short-bladed sword. Some historians say that in the first century, Emperor Titus Flavius Domitanus originated the idea of having female gladiators, know as *gladiatrices*. While apparently popular among the masses, intellectuals decried this practice, which was banned about a century after it started. Frustrated sports fans had to wait nearly two millennia to see women duking it out, as in the movie *Million Dollar Baby*.

Emperor Constantine I banned gladiator combat in 325. And although public contests occasionally took place for nearly another century, the future of gladius—the little sword—shifted to a less bloody venue, the flower garden. Enter *gladiolus*, a member of the iris family. The name is a diminutive of *gladius*, for the plant's sword-shaped leaves.

Coming in an amazing range of colors, gladioluses deservedly earned the nickname *glads*, although now we know that the word has absolutely no etymological connection to the adjective *glad*, even if the flowers make you feel that way.

gladiator & gladiolus

glamour & grammar

Grammar—the study of how words work together to make sense—can be fascinating. But few people—including grammarians—would call grammar a glamorous activity. And yet, the two words are intimately connected in terms of etymology.

Grammar traces back to the ancient Greek *gramma*, "letter," which relates to another Greek word *graphein*, "to draw or write." The gramophone, an early sound recording and playback device, was a "writer of sound."

But back to *grammar*: Over the centuries, the word took on the meaning of "learning," especially sophisticated learning. Eventually, grammar included the mastery of magic and other amazing subjects.

In the eighteenth century, as it came to denote the study of the occult, *grammar* spawned *glamour*. While *grammar* stayed behind as the term for more traditional studies, *glamour* continued its semantic evolution, eventually coming to mean things that were magical, mysterious, and, finally, in the nineteenth century, alluring.

So if you find grammar fascinating, go ahead and call it "glamorous." Even if everyone around you laughs, you'll be in the right.

God & gossip

We live at a time that could be christened "The Age of Gossip." So it makes sense to know the skinny about the word. Please keep it to yourself.

Gossip comes to us from the Old English *godsibb*, meaning a "godparent." The word is a compound formed from *God* plus *sibb*, "relative," from which we get *sibling*. Very likely the *d* was lost simply because of pronunciation, just as the *d* was lost in the pronunciation of *Wednesday*.

Originally, a gossip was a godparent of either sex. But by the fourteenth century, the word almost always referred to a woman—eventually a "godmother"—attending a birth or christening. Such an occasion was then—as it remains today—a time for exchanging news about relatives, friends, and acquaintances.

Eventually, the word *gossip* came to name not only the person gossiping but also the information disseminated. Because the most interesting news tends to be bad news, within a few centuries *gossip* came to have a negative sense. You rarely hear someone say, "I heard some good gossip about you."

Possibly if the original pronunciation had been maintained, that is, if God were still in evidence, *gossip* might not have taken such a dark turn. Maybe there wouldn't be any gossip. But given the reality of the situation, it makes sense for all of us to have a gossip defense strategy.

Will Rogers offered the following advice: "Live in such a way that you would not be ashamed to sell your parrot to the town gossip." (You do have a town gossip, right?)

If you find that suggestion difficult to implement, consider the following Spanish proverb: "Whoever gossips to you will gossip about you."

hamburger & home

Of course, there is no "ham" in hamburger. This quintessential American treat—imported from Germany—has always consisted of ground beef. The term originally was *hamburg steak*.

Just as the wiener is named for Vienna and the frankfurter is named for Frankfurt, hamburger is named for a town—Hamburg, a port city in the north of Germany. Hamburg's first syllable *ham* is from a German word meaning "village." From it English got *home* and *hamlet*. Hamburg's second syllable *burg* is German for "fortress" or "castle." Thus, Hamburg was a fortified town. English borrowed *-burg* as the suffix for many place names, such as Pittsburgh and Hattiesburg. After some twists and turns, *burg* also gave English *borough*.

But *burg* had more to offer than helping name cities. After *hamburger* became the established name for a ground beef sandwich, the word was clipped to *burger*, which then was used for any patty-like food, for example, *fish burger* and *veggie burger*.

Changing the meaning of a suffix is quite common. A familiar example is the suffix *-gate*. It was originally the final syllable in *Watergate*, the name of the Washington, DC, office and apartment complex and the location of a political burglary. After *Watergate* became the term for the offense that swept Richard Nixon from office, *-gate* took on the meaning of *scandal*, giving rise to new words such as *Irangate* and *Monicagate*.

hero &heroin

Storytellers through the ages have taught us that the hero brings hope to the masses. So what does *hero*—from a Greek word that meant "protector"—have to do with *heroin*, a substance that engenders so much hopelessness?

In 1874 a British chemist named C. R. A. Wright synthesized heroin, which proved to be ten times more powerful than morphine. Initial experiments indicated that the new painkiller was not addictive!

Before the truth came out, the drug became a big seller for the German pharmaceutical giant Bayer & Company. One use was in cough medicine for children.

Although Bayer didn't invent the drug, the company trademarked its version of the drug under the name *Heroin*. This name was chosen because of patients' statements that the "medicine" made them feel heroic.

hide & huddle

Critics have called football a brutal game. In fact, in 1905 President Theodore Roosevelt threatened to abolish the game by executive order if college administrators didn't find a way to make the play more civilized. And yet, almost from its earliest days, in addition to brawn the sport involved planning and deception.

Football—which featured a hidden-ball trick in 1903—might be called a game of "hide and seek," *hide* coming from the Old English *hydan*, "to hide," from which we get the noun *hide*, "skin," and the verb "to hoard."

The success of using secret plays led to the development of the huddle, which became a staple of the game by the early 1920s. The word *huddle*, "to crowd together," came into modern English three hundred years earlier, either from German *hudern*, "to cover or protect," or from the Old English *hydan*, "to hide."

Emma Lazarus used the adjectival form of *huddle* in her 1883 poem "The New Colossus," engraved on a plaque in the Statue of Liberty:

> *Give me your tired, your poor,*
> *Your huddled masses yearning to breathe free.*

But it was sports, not poetry, that made the word popular. Within a decade of its use on the playing field, *huddle*, meaning to bring together a small group to work out a strategy, was extended to business and other activities.

horoscope & skeptic

Skeptics tend not to believe in the possibility of gaining predictive information by studying the horoscope. But here's something they should believe: *horoscope* and *skeptic* are words of a feather. And this is their lucky day to learn all about it.

Horoscope comes from the Middle French *horoscope*, which traces back to the Latin *horoscopus*, which in turn was borrowed from the Greek compound *horoskopos*, which combined *hora*, "hour," plus *skopos*, "watching." In the context of astrology this refers to watching the hour of one's birth. According to astrologers, knowing the positions of the celestial bodies at the birth hour is critical for correctly interpreting the horoscope. At this point, our skeptic readers may be curious to know: "What's the connection between this mumbo-jumbo and us?" Here's the answer. *Skeptic*, originally used to name a member of a philosophical school existing more than two millennia ago, comes from the Greek *skeptesthai*, "to look," which traces back to *skopos*, which we just learned is the source of the second half of *horoscope*. Horoscopists fix their attention on the pattern of the stars, while skeptics use their perceptive skills to look at everything. Why do some people believe in astrology while others laugh at it? It could be a matter of when you're born . . . or not.

idiosyncrasy & idiot

Some see the assault on individuality as a by-product of the modern industrial state in which people are treated like the interchangeable parts of a machine.

In reality the negative view of eccentricity goes back much further as we will see by examining the word pair at the top of this entry.

Idiot, which in the fourteenth century was used as a label for someone with a mental deficiency, traces back not to some defect in the brain but rather to the Greek *idios*, "one's own self." The original sense was someone excessively private. The word was also applied to people lacking professional skills, a class of people who—like Edison—often surprised the world with their inventions.

The same Greek root gave rise to *idiosyncrasy*, with its primary meaning of "peculiarity," a pejorative name for a mannerism that sets a person apart from the crowd.

Of course, there have always been champions defending the rights of those who want to be idiotic. Perhaps the most celebrated example is Thoreau's entreaty: "If a man does not keep pace with his companions, perhaps it is because he hears a different drummer. Let him step to the music which he hears, however measured or far away."

And let's not overlook contemporary defenders of going it alone. As Donald N. Smith, president of Burger King, proclaimed: "The individual choice of garnishment of a burger can be an important point to the consumer in this day when individualism is an increasingly important thing to people."

impartial & umpire

"Justice," wrote Joseph Addison, "discards party, friendship, kindred, and is always, therefore, represented as blind." Baseball fans might think that Addison was also talking about the work of the unloved umpire, who is required to be impartial—and is often accused of being blind.

Impartial comes from *im-*, "not," and *partial*, "favoring one side or part." *Partial* goes back through the Old French *parcial* to the Latin *pars*, "part," the idea being that someone who is partial is taking one part over another. By not being partial, you give the same treatment to both parts.

Umpire might seem to follow the same pattern. The second part of the word—*pire*—traces back to the Old French *per*, "paired," which traces back to the Latin for "part." So if *um*, like *im-* or *un-*, means "not," then we can understand *umpire* to mean "a person who is not part of two others, hence impartial."

But the truth lies somewhere else. If you consult your dictionary, you'll discover that *um* is not a prefix. The only *um* you'll find is the interjection used to show uncertainty or to fill in the silence: "So . . . um . . . what is the *um* in *umpire*?"

Thanks for asking. *Umpire* came from the Middle English *noumpere*, "mediator," which came from the Old French *nonper*. If you needed a mediator, you'd look for "*a noumpere.*" Through a word-change process that etymologists call "misdivision" or "false splitting," over the years "*a noumpere*" came to be pronounced "*an oumpere*," ultimately giving rise to the spelling *umpire*. If this pronunciation change hadn't happened, at the ballpark you might hear fans shouting "Kill the nump." (This witty speculation comes from *The American Heritage Dictionary of the English Language, Fourth Edition.*)

infant & infantry

An *infant*—defined figuratively as "a babe in arms"—doesn't walk, whereas a member of the *infantry* is a foot soldier. Thus at first glance, it seems that *infant* and *infantry* have nothing in common. But etymologically and semantically, they are closely linked. A quotation by Frederick the Great gives a clue about the relationship. He wrote, "If my soldiers were to begin to think, not one would remain in the ranks." Frederick's words suggest that the link between *infant* and *infantry* may have to do with cognitive development.

Infant, in fact, comes from a Latin compound *infantem*, which has the same meaning as our "infant." The first syllable *in-* means "not," as in *inept*, *ineffective*, and *insincere*. But the second syllable has nothing to do with walking. Rather, *fantem* comes from the Latin verb *fari*, "to speak." Thus, an infant is a child who doesn't speak.

And infantrymen? Historically, they were the least experienced and most uneducated soldiers. Like children, they were to be seen but not heard. They were to follow orders, not dispute them. As Lord Tennyson wrote:

Theirs not to reason why,
Theirs but to do and die.

inquisition & question

Like siblings, words with the same ancestor sometimes exhibit amazingly different personalities. A perfect example is the pair that is the subject of this entry. Both *inquisition* and *question* trace back to the Latin verb *quaerere*, "to seek." Implied is the idea of entering the unknown.

It's not surprising, therefore, that so many great scholars and educators and scientists have placed questioning at the heart of their work. As Rudyard Kipling put it:

> *I keep six honest serving men.*
> *They taught me all I knew:*
> *Their names are What and Why and When*
> *And How and Where and Who.*

Ironically, from 1200 until 1800 the *Inquisition*, literally "the act of inquiring, investigating," became an anti-questioning force whose primary purpose was to promote belief.

One of the most celebrated enlightenment philosophers, Voltaire, advised: "Judge people by their questions rather than by their answers." This attitude of inquiry led him into conflict with religious dogma—beliefs that, by definition, were not to be disputed or questioned. In his book *English Letters*, Voltaire praised the freedom of thought that he found while exiled in England. That book was condemned and burned.

intermediary & media

We love the media. Which of us doesn't enjoy talking about our favorite movies, TV shows, blogs, and books? When newspapers are shut down, subscribers weep.

But we also hate the media. We condemn the electronic wasteland, castigate biased reporters, rail against entertainers who pander to the lowest common denominator, and bemoan music videos that corrupt the youth. (This negative response to the media isn't a new development. In the 1950s, Congress held hearings on horror comic books. Two thousand years earlier, Plato blamed the dramatists for endangering civilization.)

A bit of etymology can help us make sense of this. *Media* is the plural of *medium*, from the Latin *medius*, "middle," from which we get *mediocre*. But it is another relative—*intermediary*—that we must study. *Intermediary*, from the Latin *inter-*, "between," plus *medius*, "in the middle," sheds light on the media's role as go-between, whether it is bringing the muse's inspiration or God's word or news of wars or images from deep inside the human psyche.

When the media deliver unhappy or disquieting messages, it's easy to blame the messenger. But before we succumb to that temptation, we might consider George Orwell's observation: "If liberty means anything at all it means the right to tell people what they do not want to hear."

jovial & Jupiter

Many of the gods of Greek and Roman mythology were trouble-makers. For example, the scheming of Aphrodite—the goddess of love and beauty—led to the Trojan War. As a general rule, you would do best to avoid encountering the folks who called Mount Olympus home.

An exception was Jupiter, who ruled over all the other gods and who was considered a positive influence on the lives of mortals. As a bonus, Jupiter gave us the word *jovial*. Here's the story.

The Modern English *Jupiter* comes from a Latin compound *Juppiter*. *Jup* traces back to an ancient word *Jovis*, meaning "god." *Jovis* is the source of *Jove*, another name for *Jupiter*. The second half of *Juppiter—piter—*is a variation of the Latin *pater*, "father," from which we get words such as *pastor* and *paternal*. Thus *Juppiter* literally meant "god the father."

Just as English words may change their form depending on grammatical function—for example *you* becoming *your* to show possession—the possessive form of *Juppiter* was the Latin *Jovialis*, "of Jupiter." This became *jovial* in French, and that was the way the word entered English.

Originally, *jovial* referred to the many attributes possessed by Jupiter, just as the word Shakespearean refers the Bard's qualities. However, because of the widespread astrological notion that people born under the sign of the planet Jupiter would be good natured, *jovial* eventually came to mean *genial*, *happy*, and *fun loving*.

Whether people born under Jupiter's influence are generally like this is a matter outside the scope of this book. But feel free to check your chart.

karaoke & karate

Although Japan has contributed many ancient inventions to world culture, karaoke and karate are twentieth-century creations. Both, although high-energy activities, share the notion of emptiness.

Karaoke is a Japanese compound of *kara*, "empty," plus *oke*, "orchestra." *Oke* is clipped from *okesutora*, a Japanese rendering of the English *orchestra*. The literal meaning of *karaoke* is "empty orchestra." The figurative idea is that one performs to a virtual accompaniment. There are no live musicians in the orchestra pit.

Developed in the 1970s, as with most inventions karaoke had its antecedents. The idea of amateurs singing along to recorded music while reading lyrics goes back decades to when moviegoers would "follow the bouncing ball" and sing popular songs before or between feature movies. For those embarrassed by their vocal talents, such sing-alongs had the advantage of happening in the dark.

Karate is also a Japanese compound. Originally, the first word—pronounced *kara*—stood for *China*, which was where some of this martial art's practices originated. However, because of animosity between the two countries during World War II, the character for "empty"—a homonym of *China*—was substituted. The second word, *te*, means "hand." Thus, the literal meaning of *karate* is "empty hand," which figuratively suggests boxing techniques.

The worldwide appeal of karaoke and karate may come from the fact that both—unlike most popular entertainments—invite involvement. You can watch someone else perform, but it's so obvious who is having the most fun.

lace & lasso

If you play the word association game with *lace* you may come up with a word such as *frilly* or *satin*. But had you lived back in the Middle Ages, your associations might have been a bit gorier.

Lace comes from the Old French *las*, meaning "net, string," from the Latin *laqueum*, a hunting term for "noose" or "snare." The sense of "noose" may still be found in the modern English word *necklace*. The sense of "string" remains in *shoelace*. But over the centuries, *lace*'s primary meaning of "noose" faded into oblivion and was replaced by the now-familiar definition of "decorative netting" popularized in doilies and lingerie.

Meanwhile, back at the ranch (from the American Spanish *rancho*), the word *lasso* developed from an earlier Spanish word *lazo*, which came from the Latin *lacqueum*, "noose," encountered above. Although not used for hunting, the loop shape of the *lasso* pays homage to the snares used by Romans many centuries earlier.

location & locomotive

When shopping for property, many real estate agents tell their clients that the three secrets to getting value are "location, location, location." According to this witty advice, *where* you find the property is more important than what it looks like or how well built it is.

Location traces back to the Latin *locus*, "place," from which we get many words, such as *local*, *locale*, *locate*, *allocate*, *dislocate*, and one that makes real estate agents happy: *relocate*. Almost all of these *locus*-based words have a here-and-now quality that makes them easy to understand.

The exception is *locomotive*. The first part of the word, *loco*, traces back to the Latin *locus*, which we know means "place." The second part, *motive*, goes back to the Latin *motivus*, "moving," from which we get many familiar words, such as *motivate*, *mobile*, and *remove*—all involving motion. Putting the two parts of the word together creates a word meaning "moving place," seemingly an oxymoron because the first quality of a place is its immobility . . . unless you're in earthquake country.

The solution to this puzzle is revealed when we discover that *locomotive* originally was an adjective that was used only in a noun phrase and never alone. An example is *locomotive force* meaning "a force that could cause something to move from one place to another."

The modern meaning of *locomotive*—a thing that pulls or pushes railcars—was clipped from the phrase *locomotive engine* and now includes in itself the notion of an engine that supplies the place-changing force.

mailer-daemon & pandemonium

When an e-mail that you sent comes back to you from "Mailer-Daemon," this isn't the work of the devil—at least not a living, breathing devil. It's merely a message from a robotic daemon software program alerting you to the fact that there was a problem with the e-mail address.

There are many daemon programs, and if you're not aware of them, that's because they are designed to lurk silently—and invisibly—in the background, ready to handle a task if the need should arrive.

If you wonder why such a helpful type of program got such a demonic-sounding name, it's because in the 1960s the innovative computer geniuses at MIT not only were at the cutting edge of information technology, they also knew classical Greek mythology.

Specifically, they understood that in the Greek myths, daemons (pronounced just like *demons*) were helpful semi-divine beings that stood between the gods and human beings. They were the pagan equivalents of guardian angels. As such, they were the perfect model for digital servants that stood between the geeks and the end users.

But if demons are so "nice," how did they get demonized? The translators of some versions of the New Testament borrowed the word *demon* as the name for evil spirits allied with the Devil. It was that sense of the word that John Milton had in mind when, for his poem *Paradise Lost* he coined *Pandemonium* as the name of Satan's capital city, creating the word from the Geek *pan-*, "all," and *daimon*, "demon," figuratively, "a home just for demons." Knowing how evil spirits act when they get together, we can easily imagine how the word *pandemonium* came to mean chaos and mayhem.

mailer-daemon & pandemonium

maneuver & manure

Often a single root produces words that pull us in very different directions. Take the pair that title this entry.

Maneuver comes from the Old French *maneuvre*, "manual labor," which goes back to the Latin *manus*, "hand." Manual labor usually involves moving something, and by the eighteenth century *maneuver* had acquired the meaning of moving military forces. Around the same time, it also came to mean "shrewd operations" in other arenas, such as business and politics.

Manure, on the other hand, suggests something down and dirty. Also tracing back to *manus*, *manure* early on meant using hands to enrich the land with dung. Eventually the word became a synonym for dung itself.

In those old days, reviving the soil was a noble task. Indeed, until two hundred years ago, the verb *manure* was sometimes used in the sense of *develop*—so that you might talk about "manuring one's mind." Even into the twentieth century, E. B. White could comment favorably on "the smell of manure and the glory of everything."

But eventually, as the masses moved from farms to cities, they lost their appreciation of dung, so that today if you told me to "manure my writing skills," I might reply that your suggestion stinks.

menu & minute

During the next minute or two, you're going to learn that you know more than you think you do and that it takes brains to eat at a fast-food establishment. Readers, start your chronometers.

The word *minute*, referring to the unit of time, came into English from the Latin *minutus*, "small." This happened in the late fourteenth century, the beginning of the era of accurate time measurement. But the concept of the minute, as a fraction of an hour, traces back to Babylonian texts written about three thousand years earlier. The Babylonians lacked devices that could measure such small units, but they understood their theoretical importance, especially in the study of the heavenly bodies.

Menu, a French word that like *minute* traces back to the Latin *minutus*, is a nineteenth-century creation that came about to solve a practical problem: how to let restaurant customers know what items were being served—without consuming too much of the waiters' time.

The solution was to print a list of foods, known as *menu de repas*. The phrase might be translated as "a small (description) of foods." Eventually, continuing the spirit of saving space, *menu de repas* was shortened to *menu*.

We've become so used to ordering from menus that we don't realize how much knowledge and prior experience are required in the process. If you're not convinced, think about offerings such as "Big Mac" (not listed in any ordinary cookbook or dictionary).

mercenary & mercy

You could fill a thick book with spirit-lifting quotations about mercy. We have space for only a few examples:

- "I have always found that mercy bears richer fruits than strict justice."—Abraham Lincoln
- "Sweet mercy is nobility's true badge."—Shakespeare
- "Mercy and truth are met together: righteousness and peace have kissed each other."—Psalm 85

How then is it possible that a word as soulful as *mercy* can share its root with something as crass as the word *mercenary*?

Mercenary, "someone who works for money," comes from the Latin *mercenarius*, "working for pay," which traces back to the Latin *merces*, "pay," and further back to *merx*, the source of *market*. No surprises here.

But in the sixth century, there was a fork in the linguistic road. One branch, as we know, led to *mercenary*. But the other branch led to the high road, thanks to religious writers who used *merces* metaphorically to mean "the heavenly reward given to those who show compassion." This usage gave rise to the Old French *merci*, "kindness," which means "thank you" in contemporary French. And from *merci* came the English *mercy*.

Meanwhile, *Mercedes*, the Spanish word for "mercies," became a popular girl's name, which automotive innovator Emil Jellinek turned into a world-famous brand, Mercedes-Benz, thus bringing *mercy* back to its marketing roots.

message & missile

The word *missile* brings to mind images of catastrophic war while *message* suggests the peaceful gift of information. Do these seeming opposites belong in the same paragraph? You decide.

Missile comes from the Latin *missilis*, "weapon," which itself derives from the verb *mittere*, "to send." The ancient Romans sent boulders via catapult. We have the capability of sending thermonuclear devices via rocket. Different techniques, same result: a bad day for the recipient.

Message, which reached English via an Old French word, also goes back to the Latin root *mittere*. In its combining forms *mis* and *mit*, *mittere* generated many English words including *dismiss*, *emissary*, *promise*, *remittance*, *submit*, *transmission*, and *missionary*.

Unlike missiles, messages certainly can have benign purposes. For example, the very text that you are reading this instant is meant only to educate and entertain and benefit you. In no way can it harm or vaporize you.

And yet, if we are honest with ourselves, we must recognize that only the receiver is in a position to assess the effect of a message. We know this when we are on the receiving end of a comment, purportedly meant "as constructive criticism," that cuts us to the quick.

Robert Fulghum got it right when he revised the old jingle to read: "Sticks and stones will break our bones, but words will break our hearts."

mingle & mongrel

Just like human siblings, verbal relatives can have such opposite personalities you almost wonder if there was a mix-up at birth.

Mingle comes to contemporary English from the Old English *mengan*, "to mix." *Mengan*, from which we get *among*, goes further back to the hypothetical Indo-European *menq*, "to knead." The synonyms for *mingle* are almost all positive: *mix*, *blend*, *come together*, *join*, and *unite*.

The closely related *mongrel*, on the other hand, has a negative connotation. *Mongrel*, which also goes back to *menq-*, originally meant "a mixed-breed dog." But by the mid-sixteenth century, around the time of Shakespeare's birth, the word had acquired the additional meaning of "a mixed-race human being."

Although the word is rarely used in that racist sense any longer, the pejorative connotation persists even when discussing a dog's background. To avoid the derogatory label *mongrel*, animal lovers are more likely to employ the jocular term "mutt" or the neutral term "random breed."

miracle & mirror

Although the mirror was invented in antiquity and became a common household item many centuries ago, for each new generation the looking glass is a miraculous device, inspiring wonder. One can safely predict that the truth-telling mirror in the story of Snow White will never lose its quality of enchantment.

Fortunately, you don't have to be a sorcerer to explain the miraculous nature of the mirror. All it takes is a little etymological knowledge. *Miracle*, from an Old French word of the same spelling, goes back to the Latin *mirari*, "to wonder." That shouldn't surprise us because a miracle is a supernatural event designed to make witnesses wonder.

Similarly, *mirror*, which comes from the Old French *mirer*, "look at," ultimately traces back to the Latin *mirari*. Who hasn't gazed into a mirror and wondered at the image staring back?

If you happen to see a smiling expression in your reflection, that makes linguistic sense because *mirari*, the source of *mirror*, traces to the same ancient root that gives us *smile*. And for those of you who are conceited or smug, the same source also gives us *smirk*.

monster & monument

Once upon a time monsters—such as Medusa and Grendel—scared and thrilled us. So did our nightmares. Baudelaire spoke for us when he wrote, "I prefer the monsters of my fancy to what is positively trivial."

But in modern times we buy monster trucks, build monster homes, and race off to monster sales. Have we lost the true meaning of what's *monstrous* in our lives, and does it matter?

Monster comes from the Old French *monstre*, which in turn comes from the Latin *monstrum*, "monster," which referred not only to horrific creatures but also to omens, portents, and signs. *Monstrum*'s root was the verb *monere*, "to warn." Frightening creatures were symbols representing the approach of evil and doom. By paying attention, perhaps we could avoid catastrophe.

In the old days monuments provided the same benefit. *Monument*, which for us means merely a structure honoring a person, an action, or an event, originally meant something more ominous—that is, something that functions as an omen. *Monument* comes from the Latin *monumentum*, "monument," which traces back to *monere*. Hence, a monument, like a monster, had an instructive—if sometimes frightening—purpose.

So when we look at those monster homes and trucks and sales, maybe we should recall the warning of Victor Hugo: "Adversity makes men, and prosperity makes monsters."

monster & monument

month & moon

Without the moon, there would be no month. That's because a month is a unit of time based on the movements of the moon. It's 29.5 days if you use the new moon as the starting point (the synodic month); it's 27.3 days if you use celestial position (the sidereal month). Either way, it's fitting that *month* and *moon* are etymologically connected.

Month comes from the Old English *monath*, which traces back to the Latin *mensis*, "month," and back further to the Greek *mene*, "month." Etymologists speculate that the ultimate Indo-European root is *me*, the source of our word *measure*. Archeologists have found evidence that human beings were measuring moon cycles as early as the Stone Age.

Moon, from the Old English *mona*, also traces back to the Latin *mensis*, because a month is a unit of time based on the motions of the moon. From *mensis*, we get *menstruation*, a cycle that varies but on average is twenty-eight days, close enough for the name givers to associate the phenomenon with the moon cycle.

Given the moon's importance in science, myth, the arts, and personal affairs (the honeymoon), it's not surprising that our close celestial neighbor has a second name—*Luna*—a Latin word related to *lux* and *lumen*, "light," from which we get words such as *illustrate*, *lucid*, and *luminous*, plus *lunatic*, the lunar equivalent of *moonstruck*.

mortgage & mortuary

For homeowners who actually don't yet fully own their homes, the arrival of the monthly mortgage bill is as depressing as a visit to a mortuary.

And that shouldn't be a surprise, for both *mortgage* and *mortuary* are built on the Old French *mort*, meaning "dead." The French word traces back to the Latin *mori*, "to die," the ultimate source for *mortal*, which refers to any living thing that has death in its future.

Mortgage combines the idea of death with *gage*, a pledge, suggesting that if the borrower doesn't honor the pledge and pay what's due on the loan, the property will be forfeited, lost, or—metaphorically—dead to its former owner.

Other *mort* words include *mortify* (to make as if dead), *mortician* (a beautician for dead folks), and, for those who like upbeat endings, *immortality*.

mouse & muscle

Go ahead, flex your biceps. What do you see? A bump? A bulge? Maybe a mountain if you're Arnold Schwarzenegger.

To some ancient anatomist who took this same bodily Rorschach test, the rising mass of flesh must have looked like a scurrying "little mouse," hence the name *musculus*, which in Latin is the diminutive form of *mus*, "mouse."

The silent *c* makes *muscle* notoriously tricky to spell, leading countless students to wish the word were spelled like the homonym *mussel*, a delicacy whose name comes from the same root. As it happens, in Old English, the *c* in *muscle* was pronounced as a *k*—mus kle. You find an echo of this pronunciation in the word *muscular*.

We can use *muscular*—but not *muscle-bound*—in a mnemonic sentence (a memory booster) that reminds us to include a *c* in this hard-to-spell word: "If you want to be *muscular*, you have to exercise your *muscles*."

mouse & muscle

negligee & negligent

It's difficult to imagine anyone putting on a negligee in a negligent—careless—manner. After all, a negligee is surely one of the least accidental articles of clothing a person might wear. And yet there is a strong connection between *negligee* and *negligent*.

Negligent traces back to the Latin verb *neglegere*, "to ignore," a compound of *neg*, "not," plus *legere*, "to gather." *Legere* gave rise to *lecture* and *logic*, perhaps through the assumption that to speak and think coherently one must first "gather" evidence and thoughts.

Negligee, as you might guess from its sound—and meaning—comes to English from an identically spelled French word that goes back to the same Latin verb that gave rise to *negligent*. The puzzle is that "ignoring" seems to run counter to the very purpose of negligee.

But we know that etymologically—as in life—things change. So it was with *negligee*. At the time that the word was coined in the middle of the eighteenth century, wealthy women wore elaborate fashions. The negligee, at first a daytime garment, was by comparison extremely simple. A woman donning such a casual outfit was "ignoring" the elaborate conventions of the day.

A similar clothing shift happened with the tuxedo. Originally, it was casual wear designed as an alternative to the full dress coat. But as people dressed more and more casually—with businesspeople even in denim—the tux, while staying relatively unchanged in terms of its design, contextually transformed into formal attire.

nickel & Santa Claus

If ever there was a Jekyll and Hyde name, it has to be *Nicholas*.

Nicholas derives from a Greek compound of *nike*, "victory," plus *laos*, "people." From this ancient source, by way of a third-century saint, we get the name of one of history's most popular characters—*Santa Claus*—"Claus" being a contraction of the last syllables of *Nicholas*. The same source also gives us Old Nick, a name for the Devil. Exactly why people borrowed a shortened form of *Nicholas* as a name for Satan isn't known for certain, although some etymologists speculate that the choice was influenced by a hypothetical Old Norse word *nykr*, meaning "water sprite."

In any case, the Devil, in the form of Nick, also made his way into mineralogy. In the mid-eighteenth century, Swedish scientist Axel von Cronstedt isolated the element nickel from ore named *kopparnickel*, meaning "copper demon." Miners gave it that name because the ore had a copper-like appearance but contained no copper. It was a kind of fool's gold. Only in the case of kopparnickel, the disappointing ore eventually proved to be valuable when nickel became an essential ingredient in a variety of alloys. In the late nineteenth century, the U.S. mint began turning out five-cent pieces made of an alloy that was one-fourth nickel—hence the name *nickel*—and, ironically, three-fourths copper.

And if you're not into money, how about bread? *Pumpernickel* comes from a German compound of *pumpern*, "to break wind," and *nickel*, "demon." The word was originally used as an epithet for a worthless person, but we can't even offer you a half-baked theory on how the term came to be applied to something as delicious as a loaf of dark rye bread.

octagon & October

If you've taken a geometry course, you know that an octagon has eight sides, from the Greek word *okto*, "eight." The same number root gives us *octave*, the eighth full tone above a given tone; *octane*, a petroleum molecule with eight carbon atoms; and *octopus*, an eight-footed mollusk. (The octopus's feet might act like arms—especially in science fiction B movies such as *It Came from Beneath the Sea*—but the syllable *pus* comes from the Greek word *podos*, "foot," from which we get a multitude of foot words including *impediment* and *podiatrist*. This explains why octopuses are never permitted to participate in arm-wrestling competitions.)

October sure looks like one of these *okto* descendants. But it's the tenth month, not the eighth. Anyone can lose track of a day, but two months? The answer is that in the old Roman calendar, the first month was March. October was indeed the eighth month. When Julius Caesar created the new Julian calendar, January became the first month and two new months were added— April and August. This pushed October into the tenth position. November (from the Latin *nova*, "nine") became the eleventh month. And December (from the Latin *deca*) ended up in the twelfth slot.

There must have been an interesting discussion about whether or not those months with now-wrong number names should be renamed. But we couldn't get a transcript.

old & world

Although some people believe that the world was created a few thousand years ago and others set the date billions of years in the past, can't we all agree—to modify Rodney King's plea—that the world is *old*? Once we shake hands on that fact, we can enjoy the following etymology.

Old comes from an Old English word, sometimes spelled *ald*, sometimes *eald*, that originally meant "grown up." It relates to *elderly*, and, through the notion of growing tall, to *altitude*.

The connection between *old* and *world* is disguised by the fact that *world* originally was not a one-syllable word as it is today. Rather, it came to Modern English from an Old English two-syllable compound *werold*. The first syllable *wer* meant "man" and relates to the syllable *were* in *werewolf*. *Werold* literally translates "grown man" or "aged man." But the figurative meaning was the place where man has grown up. There's a parallel to the concept of "mother earth."

One might say that through the process of pronunciation change, *werold* evolved into today's *world*. But bringing evolution into the picture might upset the delicate truce we sought to establish in the first paragraph.

onion & united

In 1784 Ben Franklin wrote to a friend: "I wish the bald eagle had not been chosen as the Representative of our Country; he is a bird of bad moral Character; like those among Men who live by sharping and robbing, he is generally poor, and often very lousy." By *lousy* Ben probably meant "infested with lice" even though the word *lousy* had gained the connotation of "inferior" several centuries earlier.

Whatever Ben's intent, let's respond to his concern and nominate the onion to be the new symbol of the United States. The country's motto—*e pluribus Unum*, "from many, one"—perfectly describes the structure of the onion, which—and here's another plus—is a member of the beautiful lily family.

Like the United States, the onion consists of parts that remain separate while at the same time united to make a whole. Talk about perfect symbolism.

But if you're not yet persuaded that we should replace the eagle with the onion on our coins and banners, here comes the etymological argument: Like *united* and *union*, *onion* traces back to the Latin *unio*, meaning "unity."

Equal time requires that we give the etymology of *eagle*. It traces back to the Old French *aigle*, which comes from the Latin *acquila*, which means "eagle."

We can just hear Ben asking, "Where's the patriotic hook in that?"

opera & special ops

Stories of special ops are filled with danger, cunning, and death—just the stuff opera is made of. It's fitting, therefore, that *opera* and *special ops* are linked etymologically as well as dramatically.

For thousands of years drama has included singing. The innovation found in opera is having *all* the dialogue sung. Compared with other forms of theater, opera is a relatively modern genre, dating to the seventeenth century. But its etymology takes us far back to a source that has generated many words that exist outside the music business.

Opera came into English from an identical Italian word, *opera*, which derived ultimately from the Latin *opus*, "a work." From the same root, we get *cooperate*, *operator*, and *operation*. The French *oeuvre*, derived from the same Latin source, gave English *hors d'oeuvre*.

The phrase *special ops*—military forces trained in unconventional techniques including escape, subversion, and sabotage—is clipped from *special operations*. While the term dates from the late twentieth century, such unconventional warriors have existed throughout history. A very early example is the group, led by Odysseus, who used the Trojan horse as a ploy to enter the walled city of Troy, leading to the defeat of the Trojans. You can hear all about it in many operas, such as Berlioz's *Les Troyens*.

pasta & paste

A "rule of thumb" is an activity guide based on experience rather than rigorous experimentation. Usually, it relates to quantity. For example, the optimal number of children that should attend a party is the same as the number of years of the party giver; thus there should be five invitees to help a child celebrate a sixth birthday.

One of the best-known rules of thumb governs the cooking of pasta: "If a noodle taken from a pot of boiling pasta is thrown against a wall and if it sticks to the wall, the noodles remaining in the pot are ready to be eaten." Never having applied this rule, I can't verify its efficacy. But I can say that it gives a big clue to the etymology of the word *pasta*.

Pasta comes from the identically spelled Latin *pasta*, "dough." No matter how you shape the dough—long noodles, shells, tubes—it's still pasta.

Paste comes to English from an Old French word that, like the word referring to the foodstuff, also comes from the Latin *pasta*.

Thus when a piece of pasta adheres to a wall, it is not only telling you that it's ready to eat but is also giving you insight into its sticky etymology.

Note: If you're planning to serve pasta at a child's birthday party, reduce the number of invitees by 50 percent.

pedestal & pedestrian

Physical fitness experts agree that walking is a marvelous exercise. Maybe someone should make a statue in honor of walkers. Putting the figure of a pedestrian up on a pedestal would be a brilliant move, etymologically speaking.

Pedestrian comes ultimately from the Latin *pedis*, "foot." The *-ian* suffix is also Latin and means "a person or thing that has a relationship to whatever is named in the root of the word." Thus, a *pedestrian* is a "foot person," and by extension, "a walker." Other examples of *-ian* words include *Grecian*, *dietician*, and *reptilian*.

The use of *pedestrian* as a synonym for "ordinary" reveals the bias of upper-crust language users who had the resources to ride on horses or in horse-drawn vehicles. Easy for them to look down on walkers. Centuries later, that bias is still in effect, separating those "with wheels" from those without. Although *pedestal*, from the Italian *piedestallo*, refers to a thing, not a person, the *ped* syllable does mean "foot," used figuratively to name the base on which rests a column, statue, or some other thing. Applying body part names to name parts of objects is extremely common in many languages. English examples include the *tongue* of a shoe, an *ear* of corn, the *lip* of a pitcher.

Back to *ped*: we find this root in *pedal*, *pedicure*, and *pedicab*. But a cautionary note is in order: Several familiar *ped* words come from a completely unrelated Greek root meaning "child," for example, *pedagogy* and *pediatrician*. When it comes to etymology, assume nothing.

plastic & protoplasm

Let's try a word association game. First, what words does *plastic* bring to your mind? Second, what words does *protoplasm* make you think of?

If you're like a lot of people who played the game, your associations to these two words will be very different, the former word suggesting something hard, smooth, cold, and unbreakable and the latter something oozy, changing, warm, and alive. Yet hiding within them is a common bond.

The invention of plastic—the material that's found in thousands of products—dates from the early twentieth century. But the word itself—meaning something that can be shaped—is more than four hundred years old. Ultimately, it traces back to the Greek *plastikos*, "moldable," from the verb *plassein*, "to mold." This may not sound all that exciting, but one of the most memorable movie lines comes at the beginning of *The Graduate* when Benjamin (played by Dustin Hoffman) is told the one word he needs to know to succeed in life: "Plastics."

Speaking of life: *Protoplasm*, a mid-nineteenth century word, came into English from the German *protoplasma*, coined by a botanist from two Greek elements—*proto-*, "first," plus *plasma*, "something molded," which is derived from the verb *plassein*, "to mold."

So what we have here are two substances—one synthetic and the other living—that can be molded into seemingly endless shapes and for uncountable purposes.

polish & polite

The word *polite* is a powerful stimulant for aphorists. Thomas Jefferson wrote: "Be polite to all but intimate with few." Madame de Staël called politeness "the art of choosing among your thoughts." And Winston Churchill explained, "When you have to kill a man, it costs nothing to be polite."

But it is Colette who comes closest to pegging the etymology of the word, when she advises that we "apply the oil of refined politeness to the mechanisms of friendship." If Colette's image brings to mind a woodworker finishing a piece of furniture, and if in turn that suggests the nineteenth-century institution known as the "finishing school," you're on the right track.

Polite comes to us from the Latin *politus*, literally "polished," which traces back to the verb *polire*, "to make smooth." Originally, *polite* was used as a synonym for *polish*, which derives from the same Latin root. Then, by metaphorical extension, *polite* came to mean "refined, elegant."

But watch out! If you're too smooth, instead of seeming polite you may come across as slick or even oily.

posse & possible

Can today's superstars surrounded by their posses be in the dark about the etymology of *posse*? As Samuel Goldwyn put it: "In two words: *im possible.*" But just in case, let's shed some light on the matter.

Starting with the second part of Mr. Goldwyn's solecism, we learn that *possible* comes from the Latin *posse*, literally, "to be able." Implicit in *posse* is the notion of having power. Hence, from the same root we get *potent, potential,* and *potentate,* of which movie mogul Samuel Goldwyn is a handy example.

At this point, you've probably guessed that the English word *posse*—an ad hoc band of deputized citizens seen in so many cowboy pictures—hearkens back to the Latin word *posse.* It does, but the story has a few twists and turns.

In the Middle Ages, the Latin word *posse* combined with another Latin word *comitatus,* "county," to form the phrase *posse comitatus,* in essence, a community police force. We're talking about the sort of rag-tag group that the Sheriff of Nottingham might have gathered to pursue Robin Hood.

Later, through the same process of clipping that turned *principal teacher* into *principal* and *private soldier* into *private,* the phrase *posse comitatus* was abbreviated to *posse.* The word got lots of use in the American Wild West.

With the closing of the frontier, the term was largely abandoned. But the rise of celebrities—more powerful than sheriffs even—resurrected the word. Now no self-respecting superstar goes about without a *posse,* also known as an *entourage.* Would you? Im possible.

praise & price

One of Madison Avenue's weirdest semantic contributions to American culture—right up there with "I'm not a doctor but I play one on TV"—is the phrase "as advertised on television." It's not strange that advertisers pay to persuade us. What's incredible is that they would brazenly cite a paid advertisement as if it could have any informational value for a consumer. More astounding: the technique works!

After we take our hats off to the copywriters, and hand them our wallets, we wonder what could have inspired them to try such an outrageous strategy. The answer may be found in the etymology of the two words that title this entry.

Praise, which is at the heart of every advertisement—whether it's singing the virtues of a friendly bank or a brand of soft drink—comes from the Old French *preisier*, "to praise, to value," which came from the Latin *pretium*, the source of several modern English words including *precious* and *prize*. Nothing surprising so far.

But then we discover that *price*, going back through the Old French *pris*, "value," also traces back to *pretium*. It's a small step from that linguistic coincidence to the realization that praise can be had for a price, which brings us back to Madison Avenue.

president & sedentary

The title of this entry isn't meant to demean the office of the President of the United States. We're simply stating an etymological fact: There's a connection between being president and being sedentary, and it's more than that big leather chair in the Oval Office.

The thesaurus suggests many verbs describing what the president does: *lead*, *command*, *manage*, *organize*, *budget*, *inspire*, and of course *preside*.

Sit isn't on the list, but when we look closely at *preside*, we discover that it comes from the Latin *praesidere*, literally "sit before"—a compound that traces back to *sedere*, "to sit." The first syllable *sed* gives us a clue that *sedentary* also arises—so to speak—from *sedere*. So the president is a sitter.

But don't take the etymologist's word for it. Here's what Harry Truman, the thirty-third president, said about the job: "I *sit* here all day trying to persuade people to do the things they ought to have sense enough to do without my persuading them."

Given that *president* etymologically means "someone who sits," we're forced to conclude that the widely used phrase "sitting president" is a redundancy. But being redundant is hardly the nastiest label said about the job. While serving as president, Thomas Jefferson wrote: " . . . it brings nothing but increasing drudgery and daily loss of friends."

prison & reprehensible

When we hear that someone has been sent to prison, quite often the person proves to be reprehensible. Think of Al Capone, who once said, "You can get much farther with a kind word and a gun than you can with a kind word alone." This kind of person deserves to be censured, punished, and—of course—rehabilitated.

It thus seems just that, etymologically speaking, *prison* and *reprehensible* are joined at the root. *Prison* goes back the Latin *prehendere*, "to take, to capture." If you're in prison, it means that you have been taken, like a piece in a chess match.

Reprehensible also goes back to *prehendere*. The prefix *re-* means "back," so that a *reprehensible* person is someone who has been taken back, recaptured, not a first-time offender.

Of course, there's also the hope of reprieve. It too comes from *prehendere*, which seems odd given that its meaning suggests something positive while its etymology suggests something negative—being "recaptured." This puzzle is solved when we learn that *reprieve* originally meant "being sent back to prison as an alternative to beheading." Most prisoners would agree that while incarceration is bad, it's less bad than death.

Prolific *prehendere* also gives us the word *surprise*. When the prefix *sur-*, meaning "over" combines with *prehendere*, you get the expression "to overtake." If you pursue and overtake someone— say an escaped convict—the person is surprised, literally "over taken." The word later expanded to mean any unexpected occurrence . . . like a reprieve.

proud & prude

Proud—a Jekyll and Hyde word, sometimes positive, other times negative—came into English from the Old French *prud*, "brave." The word traces back to the Latin *prodesse*, "to be useful." We see this affirmative meaning in a quotation such as:

> "I like to see a man proud of the place in which he lives.
> I like to see a man live so that his place will be proud of him."
>
> —ABRAHAM LINCOLN

Although the word still is used in that sense—for example, in bumper stickers that proclaim "Proud to be _____" (fill in the blank), by Shakespeare's time *proud* had also acquired the sense of being "full of oneself, conceited." For example:

> "A proud man is seldom a grateful man, for he never thinks he gets as much as he deserves."
>
> —HENRY WARD BEECHER

Pride, which is closely related, has the same negative take in the title of Jane Austen's *Pride and Prejudice*.

Prude traces back to the Old French *preude*, "virtuous," a relative of *prud*. But in English, by the 1700s its negative meaning—"excessively proper"—was completely dominant.

Now you know why you will not likely encounter a bumper sticker reading "I'm a prude and proud of it."

pupil & puppet

The theme of this entry is: "Small is beautiful." Or if not beautiful, at least "cute."

Let's start with *pupil*, the small, blackish circle in the middle of the eye. When you stare into someone else's pupil, you see a tiny version of yourself. Early Roman anatomists had the same experience, which is why they named that reflective part of the eye the *pupilla*, "little doll." The meaning of *pupil* as a student traces back to the same root, the notion being that a student is a little person.

Puppet—another example of linguistic "smallification"— comes from the Old French *poupette*, the diminutive of *poupee*, "doll." Poupee goes back to the Latin *pupa*, "girl." Incredibly, by the mid-sixteenth century, just a few years after it came to name the figure or doll manipulated in a theatrical performance, the word *puppet* had acquired the secondary meaning of a human being controlled by someone else. Now, if we had taken to heart Ralph Waldo Emerson's warning that "A foolish consistency is the hobgoblin of little minds," we might have daringly included a third item in the title of this entry—*puppy*—whose etymology closely parallels that of *pupil* and *puppet*. We would have described how *puppy* came from the Middle French *poupee*, "doll," eventually replacing the native word for young dog, *whelp*.

But being less adventurous than Emerson, we didn't make the title "pupil & puppet & puppy" so please forget that you read the previous paragraph.

quintessence & quintuplets

This entry is for anyone who likes the number five, or wild goose chases, or long odds, or all of the above.

More than two thousand years ago, Aristotle speculated that the universe didn't consist only of the four known elements—earth, air, fire, and water. He proposed that there was a fifth element, the "ether" that was part of all things. In Greek, he called this substance *pempte ousia*, which the Romans translated as *quintessence*, from the Latin *quintus*, "fifth," plus *essentia*, "fundamental substance."

Of course, the traditional four elements eventually proved not to be elemental at all. Thus in hindsight, it's not surprising that the alchemists searched in vain for the quintessence. But the word itself survived, used most often in its adjectival form, referring to the purest or most representative instance of a thing, for example: "Othello is the quintessential jealous husband."

Quintuplets, which is a diminutive formed from *quintuple*, comes ultimately from the Latin *quintus*, "fifth." Human quintuplets—five children born to the same mother at the same time—are almost as rare as Aristotle's hypothetical element. Before the advent of modern fertility methods, the odds against giving birth to quintuplets were calculated to be about 65 million to 1. When the Dionne quintuplets were born in 1934—and all five survived—the event was covered in newspapers throughout the world. Although the arrival of quintuplets is hardly commonplace, in recent years there have been instances of sextuplets and septuplets surviving.

Impressive to us humans but not to opossums, which may give birth to twenty offspring. Would those babies be called *vigintlets*? (A Latin dictionary is never around when you need it.)

radical &radish

The first written instance of *radical*—referring to political reform—came in the eighteenth century. The notion of *extremist* reform arrived soon after when the term was applied to the far-left wing of the British Liberal party.

In the United States during the 1960s and 1970s, radical antiwar groups such as the Weathermen went underground when targeted by the authorities. Perhaps unconsciously, the radicals were not only seeking sanctuary but also returning to their etymological roots. *Radical* came into English from the Late Latin *radicalis*, "having roots," which in turn came from the Latin *radix*, "radish."

When the authorities tried to eradicate the radicals—*eradicate* deriving from the Latin *eradicare*, "root out"—they were in the same lexicological territory, because—is it too obvious to point out?—*eradicare* is itself derived from *radix*.

Politics does make strange bedfellows—especially if we're talking about a vegetable bed.

read & riddle

Can you figure out the connection between *read* and *riddle*? If you want a clue, there's one in the first sentence.

A riddle is an ultra-short mystery in which the text contains the clues needed to find the solution. For example: You walk up to someone and say, "Everything I tell you is a lie." Are you telling the truth or are you lying?

We'll get to the answer soon, but while you're thinking about it, let's look at the etymology of *riddle*. *Riddle* comes from the Old English *raedels*, "conjecture." The purpose of the riddle is to make the audience think. *Raedels* traces back to the hypothetical Indo-European root *ar* from which came *arithmetic*, *rational*, and *reason*.

Read, meanwhile, comes from the Old English *raedan*, "to explain," which also traces back to the *ar-* root. We discover, therefore, the reading isn't merely decoding letter sounds, but rather thinking about texts. Thus, riddling can be seen as simply a special case of reading.

Now, before you read the answer to the riddle: Did you think about it yourself? Did you exercise your brain? If not, take another look at the riddle. If yes, you may proceed to the next paragraph.

The answer to the riddle is: You're lying. Here's how we know. If you were telling the truth about always lying, then you wouldn't always be lying. So that would make a contradiction. But if you're lying when you say, "Everything I tell you is a lie," there's no contradiction. You've just told a lie, but that doesn't mean you *always* lie. Everyone tells the truth sometimes, right?

rectitude & rectum

Rectitude suggests many things—honesty, morality, goodness, correctness, decency, integrity. But *rectum* is probably not on the list. And yet, etymologically, the two words couldn't be closer.

Both derive from the Latin *rectus*, meaning "straight," from which we get *rectangle*, with its straight sides. That geometric figure seems to fit a person of rectitude, a person who is upright and foursquare. A public person who can withstand scrutiny.

But what about the rectum? For those of you who haven't done an autopsy lately, the facts are these: Unlike the curvaceous part of the intestines, also known as the small intestines, the rectum is the straight part of the bowels. And that straightness is a good thing when it's time to use a rectal thermometer.

room & rummage

When you run out of room for your stuff and you decide it's the perfect time for a rummage sale, your etymological intuition may be what's inspiring you, for the two words—*room* and *rummage*—are closely connected.

Rummage, which today means "odds and ends," and also "to search for something by going through those odds and ends," comes from the Middle French word *arrumage*, "arrangement of cargo in a ship's hold." *Arrumage* itself traces back to the word *rum*, which referred to a ship's hold.

Old English had a related word *rum*, which referred to the space in a home. That word competed for a while with the French word *chamber*—which gave English *chamber pot*, *gas chamber*, and *chamber music*. Eventually, *rum*—in the form of *room*—won out, so now we have dining rooms, living rooms, bedrooms, and even great rooms.

But it seems that there's never enough room, which fact led to the nineteenth-century invention of the rummage sale, which etymologically might be translated as "room-making sale." The first rummage sale was, appropriately enough, dreamed up by a shipping company to get rid of unclaimed goods from a ship's *rum*. Now, of course, we hold rummage sales to raise money for worthy causes by getting rid of our unwanted possessions so that we can make room for new things that eventually can be turned into rummage. And so it goes.

In selling our treasures, we might also be motivated by what some authorities say are the last words of Elizabeth I: "All my possessions for a moment of time."

sad & satisfaction

If you can't "get no satisfaction," maybe you have a right to feel sad.

But with that exception understood, why in the world are these two polar opposites—*sad* and *satisfaction*—hanging together?

An aphorism by novelist Edna Ferber gives us a clue: "Perhaps too much of everything is as bad as too little."

Sad came into modern English from the Old English *saed*, "full," from a hypothetical Proto-Indo-European word *seto*, "satisfied." Over time, *sad* acquired the meaning of "heavy, tired," suggesting the feeling one gets when having more than enough, being glutted. Eventually, the related word *sated* acquired the sense of being overstuffed, at which point *sad* continued its downward emotional journey, becoming a synonym for *unhappy* and *sorrowful*.

Satisfaction, meanwhile, came into English from the Latin *satisfactionem*, originally, "an act performed by a church person to atone for sin." *Satisfactionem* traced back to the Latin *satis*, "enough," itself derived from *seto*. Possibly the spiritual nature of the act of satisfaction protected the word's positive meaning, making it unlikely that anyone who got *satisfaction* would find it excessive and sad.

In the interest of fairness, though, we will allow Mae West to attack the idea that excess is a downer. Mae famously proposed that "too much of a good thing is wonderful."

salad & salary

English contains many synonyms for the payment received in exchange for work: *compensation, earnings, emolument, fee, honorarium, remuneration, stipend,* and *wages.* Of course, the words are not perfectly interchangeable. While money is money, a plumber is not likely to ask for an honorarium, although snaking out the pipes is just as honorable as, say, giving a speech.

A word that has wider application is *salary,* and it definitely has a more interesting etymology. *Salary* comes from the Latin *salarium,* figuratively "pay," and literally "pertaining to salt." The term originally meant "money paid to a Roman soldier for the purchase of salt rations." Obviously, in those days, salt was considered a precious substance.

Salarium traces back to the hypothetical Indo-European root *sal,* which was the source of many salty words. These include *salsa, sauce, sausage, salami,* and *salad,* which was clipped from the Latin phrase *herba salata,* "salted vegetables." So if you eat your salad without adding salt, in a sense you're not eating a salad at all.

salon & saloon

Salon brings to mind the Enlightenment era, with its elegant Parisian rooms, where one might find great musicians, painters, poets, authors, and philosophers engaged in brilliant conversations and displays of virtuosity, such as Chopin launching his career in 1832 in one of Pleyel's salons.

Saloon, on the other hand, suggests a setting for crooked gamblers, drunks, bullies, gunslingers, player pianos, prostitutes (with hearts of gold), and . . . ham sandwiches:

> A ham sandwich goes into a saloon and says, "Bartender, I need a drink." And the bartender replies, "Sorry, we don't serve food here."

As different as these two words seem, they are kissing cousins etymologically speaking. *Salon*, borrowed directly from a French word for "reception room," also has roots to an Old English word, *sele*, "hall."

Saloon was originally simply an Anglicized version of *salon*—pronounced differently but with the identical meaning. Transported from England to America in the middle of the nineteenth century it became a synonym for a drinking establishment, especially catering to the sort of people who didn't frequent salons.

salon & saloon

sanction & sanctuary

The words *sanction* and *sanctuary* bring to mind Robert Frost's image of two roads diverging. Starting from the same root, these words represent amazingly different etymological paths—the former leading to punishment, the latter protection.

Sanction has many meanings, all based on the notion that a recognized authority has the power to control behavior, even to the point of employing coercive measures, such as one nation blockading shipments to another. The word goes back to the Latin *sanctio*, "decree," which leads further back to *sancire*, "make sacred," also the source of *saint*. *Sancire* was first used in connection with religious edicts, but with the rise of secular governments, its verbal offshoot—*sanction*—was applied to nonreligious laws. Although the source of power was different—social rather than theological—the effect was the same: those who disobeyed the law would be punished.

The religious roots of *sanctuary* are more obvious because the word refers to a physical reality that still exists: church buildings. The word goes back to the Middle Ages when it was first used to name a place set aside for worship. Thus it was a synonym for the much earlier Greek-derived *church*.

In the Middle Ages, religious law gave fugitives who entered a sanctuary protection from civil authorities seeking to arrest them. This use of the church as a safe haven gave the word *sanctuary* its extended meaning as any place that provided relief from physical or psychological danger.

By the twentieth century, embassies had acquired this function, a tradition that was infamously disrespected when, in 1972, Iranians invaded the U.S. Embassy in Tehran.

sand & sandwich

Kids sometimes call it "samwich," perhaps because they can't believe there's sand in it. But in fact there is *sand* in *sandwich*, at least etymologically.

The sandwich was named after John Montagu, Fourth Earl of Sandwich, an eighteenth-century British aristocrat. Although he didn't dream up the idea of eating food held between two slices of bread, legend has it that Lord Sandwich was fond of this form of eating while he was playing cribbage. This way his hands wouldn't get the cards sticky. The idea of pressing meat or other fillings between the bread slices led, through metaphorical extension, to the sense of being squashed, as when a football quarterback is sandwiched between two tacklers.

As for the sand in our story? John Montagu's title—Earl of Sandwich—came from the place he lived, the village of Sandwich in the county of Kent. Located on the English Channel and thus having a beach, Sandwich took its name from two Old English words—*sand* plus *wic*, "place." In its modern form, *wich* is found in many place names such as Greenwich and Ipswich.

The important thing to remember from all this is that John Montagu didn't invent the sandwich, just as Joseph Guillotin didn't invent the guillotine. These men simply were in favor of the items for which they are remembered. The moral: Be careful what you recommend.

sarcasm & sarcophagus

Some people classify sarcasm as a form of humor. But those on the receiving end more likely view this form of mockery as violence. And etymologists support that point of view.

Let's start with sarcasm's close relative, *sarcophagus*, an elaborately ornamented tomb that, in ancient Rome and Greece, was often made of limestone. *Sarcophagus* comes from the Greek *sarkophagos*, a compound made up of *sarkos*, "flesh," plus *phagous*, "to eat." The tomb earned its name—"eater of flesh" because the lime in the limestone accelerated the decomposition of the body.

From *phagous* we get the second half of *anthropophagy*, an erudite synonym for *cannibalism*.

Now we should be in the proper mood for *sarcasm*, which goes back to the Greek *sarkasmos*, "a sneer," which is bad enough, the kind of thing that made silent movie audiences hiss at the villain. But it gets worse. When you trace *sarcasm* further you come to *sarkazein*, with the literal meaning "to strip off the flesh." We encountered the first syllable—*sark*—in the root of *sarcophagus*. And if we go back one more step, we come to a hypothetical Proto-Indo-European root *twerk*, "to cut."

There is no question that the purpose of sarcasm is to wound. So the next time you are tempted to use it, remember the observation of Thomas Carlyle: "Sarcasm I now see to be, in general, the language of the devil; for which reason I have long since as good as renounced it."

sauté & somersault

For children, doing a somersault is not only a fun thing to do, but also a symbol of growing up, like figuring out how to tie a shoelace or ride a two-wheeler. For etymologists, who perhaps have forgotten the first time they went head-over-heels, the word *somersault* is a "corruption," meaning that its pronunciation has been altered so much from its source that the true etymological links are difficult to spot.

Somersault, indeed, has nothing to do with summer or with salt. The word tumbled—or stumbled—into English from the Middle French *sombresault*, which came ultimately from two Latin words *supra*, "over," plus *saut*, "jump."

Perhaps a French chef, having just returned from an exciting day at the circus, decided to borrow the idea of jumping to describe the method of cooking foods in a hot pan. That's speculation, but we do know for a certainty that *sauté*, "jumped," which comes from the Latin *saltare*, "to hop," was the word used to describe what happens to the items that the cook flips up and over, making it seem—for example—as if a piece of pepper or chicken were doing a somersault.

scintilla & scintillate

It's hard to imagine a pair of words so alike in structure and so different in meaning.

Scintillate comes from the Latin *scintillare*, "to sparkle," which in turn comes from the noun *scintilla*, "glittering speck." Used literally, it brings to mind fireworks throwing out shows of colorful embers. Used figuratively, it suggests the kind of brilliant behavior that makes celebrities stand out.

Via metathesis—the rearranging and dropping of letters—in the fifteenth century the same root gave rise to *tinsel*—precious fabric interwoven with glittering gold threads. However, as the centuries passed, *tinsel* lost some of its splendor, and came to mean gaudy. In the 1970s, it became part of Hollywood's nickname—*Tinseltown*—suggesting sham showiness that somehow still was able to turn heads and dazzle crowds.

And then from the same sparkling Latin source, but without any of *scintillate*'s brilliance or tinsel's pizzazz, came *scintilla*, "the smallest part, the least trace." *Scintilla* is used almost always negatively, as in "not a scintilla of proof."

How did a word with such a bright past end up so far down in the dumps?

senate & senile

You might think that the framers of the Constitution were careless in calling the upper chamber of Congress the *senate*, a term related to *senile*. Both words derive from the Latin *senex*, "old man."

But a bit of word sleuthing shows us that the founders were blameless, at least in this connection. In the seventeenth century, *senile* simply referred to someone old or senior. Back then, elder statesmen were held to be sources of wisdom. It wasn't until the mid-nineteenth century that *senile* acquired the meaning of "weak or infirm from age."

And what constitutes "old" in connection with serving in the U.S. Senate? The minimum age according to the Constitution is thirty years, five years more than the minimum age for serving in the House of Representatives.

There have been, however, several exceptions. The youngest person ever to serve in the Senate was John Eaten, who in 1818 was sworn in at the age of twenty-eight. Apparently, Eaton himself was not aware of his true age until much later in his life.

shirt & skirt

Anyone who has ever seen a shirt and a skirt has a right to be puzzled by this pairing. Although the two words look and sound alike, the garments they name have nothing in common. One covers the top part of the body, the other the bottom. One has sleeves, the other doesn't. There's even a gender difference, with the skirt being almost universally female clothing.

So what then is the etymological connection? The answer has to do with the eternal truth that fashion never stands still, at least not women's fashion.

Our story begins with the Old English *scyrte*, "tunic" (short coat). *Scyrte*, which eventually acquired the modern pronunciation of *shirt*, traces back to a hypothetical ancient German word that gave rise to the English *short*. All this makes sense because a shirt, if anything, is short.

Meanwhile, *skirt* entered English from the Old Norman *skyrta*, which—like it's Old English counterpart—also meant "shirt." *Skyrta*, according to some authorities, applied to a long style of peasant shirt. When this long garment moved downward to the waist, the name remained, as it did centuries later as the skirt shortened upward, eventually giving rise in the 1960s to the miniskirt, a term eventually shortened to *mini*, which—as the garment continued to diminish—paradoxically lengthened to the *micromini*.

snooty & snotty

In terms of functionality, the human nose plays a minor part in human affairs. While the perfume industry always does good business, when it comes to using smell for survival, people rely on animals, for example, bomb-sniffing dogs.

But if we're talking about appearances, then the human nose matters. We know this from literature—the story of Cyrano. We know this from the statistics on rhinoplasty (nearly 200,000 "nose jobs" done each year in the United States). And we know this from the two words atop this entry.

Snooty is a twentieth-century coinage, although the kind of condescending attitude that it suggests has to be timeless. The *snoot* part of the word is a Scottish dialectical version of *snout*, which traces back to the Middle Low German and Middle Dutch *snute*, "snout." Although originally the word referred to the nose of an animal, eventually it was applied to the human nose, especially to a nose that was prominent.

Snute also spawned the German *Schnauze*, from which came *schnauzer*, a type of dog, and also from which came the Yiddish *shnoitsl*, which gave rise to the Americanized *schnoz*, a playful synonym for nose made popular by Jimmy Durante, the vaudeville, film, and TV star who referred to his own large nose as a *schnozzola*.

Snotty traces back to an Old English word *gesnot*, "snot," or more politely "nasal mucus." It's easy to imagine how a word labeling the stuff from the nose might eventually be applied to the owner of the stuff, and then to anyone—even a dry-nosed person—who was as unappealing as nose mucus. We see the exact same development with other bodily products, but let's not go into that.

snooty & snotty

stupendous & stupid

You don't need a high IQ to predict that *stupid* is an old word. People have been stupid forever. In the 1980s Hewlett-Packard turned down a chance to own the Apple computer business . . . for free. Sixty years before that, a *New York Times* editorial "explained" why rockets can't work in the vacuum of outer space. In the same period Thomas Edison called radio "a fashion contrivance that will soon die out." A few centuries earlier church leaders threatened to burn Galileo for saying that the earth moved.

It was around Galileo's time that *stupid* entered English, coming from the Latin *stupere*, "stunned," ultimately from a hypothetical Indo-European root meaning "hit." In other words, people who appear stupid may act that way not because they lack sufficient gray matter but because they are knocked senseless—figuratively speaking—by the events in their lives.

And this brings us to *stupendous*, which might appear to be a modern Madison Avenue coinage cut from the same cloth as *truckathon* and *sale-a-bration*. But in fact, *stupendous* is nearly as old as *stupid* and traces back to the same Latin verb. It refers to something capable of stunning people, but with the twist of evoking wonder. A small difference. A stupendous difference.

tax & taxi

Some words that look alike—for example, *police* and *polite*—prove to have no etymological connection. But the fact that *tax* and *taxi* share the notion of payment encourages us to guess that they are words of a feather. And in fact, they are, although one is ancient and the other modern.

Tax, of course, goes back to the dawn of history. Even before money was in use governments collected taxes in the form of labor. The word *tax* comes from the Latin *taxare*, "to assess," and ultimately derives from the verb *tangere*, "to touch." We can see the connection between taxing and touching in the familiar phrase "to touch someone up for a loan."

Taxi is a far younger word. Although the business of hiring a driver dates at least from the horse-drawn carriage era in seventeenth-century Paris, the taxi story begins in 1891 when Wilhelm Bruhn invented the *taximeter*, a device that automatically calculated fares based on distance and time.

Bruhn's device was imported to France where it was installed first in a type of electric vehicle known as a *taximeter cab*. The second word in the phrase is a clipped form of *cabriolet*, originally a horse-drawn carriage. The carriage, whose suspensions bounced passengers up and down, got its name from the Latin *capreolus*, "wild goat," from which we get the word *caper*.

When taximeter cabs were imported into the United States, the name was clipped to *taxicab*, which later split into *taxi* and *cab*.

The industrial-age passion for accuracy as seen in Bruhn's taximeter gave rise forty years later to Carl Magee's invention of the parking meter. Magee's widely despised device made it possible to charge people whether they are moving or immobile.

tenacious & tenant

Landlord/tenant interactions are occasionally difficult. They've even led to uprisings, such as the "Anti-Rent War" of the mid-nineteenth century. Perhaps a bit of etymology can lead both sides to domestic tranquility.

Landlords should not be surprised if a tenant tenaciously seeks to remain in a property. The word *tenant* goes back about a thousand years to the identically spelled Old French *tenant*, which comes from the Latin *tenere*, "to hold." The same Latin root gave us several English words including *tenure*, the right to hold a job under certain defined circumstances; *tenet*, a belief that a person holds to be true; and *lieutenant*, an officer who holds the place of (that is, represents) someone higher in the command chain. (Americans say *lieutenant* pretty much as the French do, the syllable *lieu*, "place," being pronounced as "loo." Why the British pronounce the word "lef-tenant" is a mystery, but it is a practice that is strongly maintained.)

Ah, but *maintain*, another "holding" word—from the Latin *manu tenere*, literally "to hold in the hand" and figuratively "to keep up"—brings us back to *tenant* and the tenant's occasional tenacious behavior. *Tenacious*, like *tenant*, goes back to the Latin *tenere*, "to hold." What then could be more natural for a tenant—a "place holder"—to be tenacious, that is, to try to hold onto a property, especially if it's well maintained.

tenderfoot & tent

Of all the word pairs in this book, the bond between *tenderfoot* and *tent* brought me the biggest smile and led to the greatest surprises.

Originally, this entry was to be "tendon & tent." I was interested in tendons because a relative had suffered a bad case of tendonitis. *Tendon*, I learned, goes back to the Latin *tendere*, "to stretch." We know what happens when tendons overstretch. From there, it was easy to guess that *tent*, made by stretching material over a frame, might have an etymological connection. It does. *Tent* comes to English from the Old French *tente*, "tent," which comes from the Middle Latin *tenta*, "tent," which come from *tendere*, the verb we met above.

So that's the story I was prepared to share when it occurred to me that *tension* might be another stretch word. It is, and when I traced it back to the hypothetical Indo-European *ten*, "stretch," that made me want to find out other words in the family. There are a lot more than I imagined. These include: *intense*, *pretend*, *pretensions*, *tendency*, *tensile*, *tenterhooks*, and . . . *tender*.

Tender was at first a puzzle, because it suggests the quality of "soft" and "fragile," whereas something that is stretched can be "tight as a drum." But then I recalled my relative's tendonitis, and how sensitive he was to the lightest touch.

From *tender* it's just a step to *tenderfoot* and the image of young scouts stretched out in their first tents.

testicle & testimony

There's a fascinating legend about this pair of words. It's a blend of fact and fancy that goes like this:

Fact: *Testicle*, "the male sex gland that secretes spermatozoa," traces back to the Latin *testis*, "testicle."

Fact: *Testimony*, "evidence," traces back to the Latin *testis*, which in addition to "testicle" meant "witness."

Fancy: Some writers concluded that there was a direct relationship between the words. The relationship was based on the belief that a Roman man testifying in court had to place his hand on his testicles as a sign that he was telling the truth, just as we, today, might place a hand over the heart. Hence, *testimony* and *testify* were thought to be related to *testicle*.

The only problem is that no one has brought forth any evidence that Romans used their testicles to indicate truthfulness. There is an Old Testament reference to Jews following the practice, but nothing connects the Biblical text to Roman culture.

One theory about what's going on here is that *testis* represents two unrelated words, just as the English *bear* refers both to an animal and to the act of carrying something. According to this theory, one of the *testis* words simply named the male sex gland. There is some evidence that the other *testis* traced back to an ancient word meaning "a third person," hence a neutral witness. This second *testis* gave rise to the Latin *testificare*, "to witness," which eventually evolved into *testify* but which had nothing to do with touching one's testis or testicles or . . . anything else.

The legend, which is so graphic, makes for better reading than the theory. But this is a work of nonfiction, and the author has sworn to tell the truth, the whole truth, and nothing but the truth . . . so far as he knows it.

thank & think

"Good manners will open doors that the best education cannot," advises Supreme Court Justice Clarence Thomas. That's why we work hard to teach children to say "Thank you." But if etymologists are to be believed, there's an additional benefit: developing the intellect. Here's the story.

Thank you goes back to the fifteenth century, when the phrase was clipped from the more complete "I thank you." The operative word *thank* traces back centuries more to the Old English *thancian*, which included the sense of being thoughtful. The modern English *think* comes from the exact same root. We can speculate, then, that those early English speakers felt that expressing appreciation for something—being thankful—required an act of thinking.

Our own experience tells us that this is so, especially when we're not on autopilot and sending prewritten thank-you cards. When we want to thank someone for a gift, the phrase "thank you" is less important than the details we add that describe our perception of the gift and why we value it.

So when we ask our kids to compose thank-you notes for the gifts or favors they receive, we are actually teaching them how to think. Don't expect them to thank you for this, but if they need additional motivation, remind them what George Bernard Shaw wrote: "Few people think more than two or three times a year. I have made an international reputation for myself by thinking once or twice a week."

theater & theory

In 1959, novelist and physicist C. P. Snow published *The Two Cultures and the Scientific Revolution*, a controversial book that deplored the growing gap between science and the humanities. Snow believed that solving the world's problems required improved communication and understanding between the two forms of knowledge.

Increasing specialization since the publication of Snow's book has perhaps widened the gulf. This entry modestly seeks to bridge it in at least one place.

The word *theater* comes to English through the Old French *theatre*, which traces back to the Greek *theatron*, from *thea*, "a view," plus *-tron*, a suffix denoting "place." It is a place for viewing life. The synonym *stage*, from the Latin *statum*, conveys much the same meaning: a place where the action will occur.

Although *theory* suggests something abstract, its etymology reveals that—like theater—it is rooted in observation. Theory, which plays such a key role in scientific progress, comes from the Greek *theoria*, "speculation," which in turn comes from *theoros*, "spectator," which comes from *thea*, which we learned means "a view." (Note that speculation itself relates to perception, coming from the Latin *specere*, "to look at.")

So we can give the same advice to any wannabe playwright or Einstein: Keep your eyes open . . . and your mind, too.

tornado *&* tortuous

We like it when we can trace a word in a straight, unbroken line to its source and thereby illuminate the present and the past. *Curfew* is that kind of word. We trace it back to an Old French compound *covrefeu*, consisting of *couvrir*, "to cover," plus *feu*, "fire." We get the idea that in the old days, when the fire was put out, it was time to hit the hay. End of story. Next word.

Unfortunately, as you might expect from its real-world behavior, *tornado* doesn't follow a direct etymological path. But if you're willing to follow a tortuous path, come along.

Tortuous is a well-behaved word that comes from the Latin *tortuous*, "full of twists," derived the Latin *torquere*, "to twist." From *torquere* we get *torture*, originally, imposing pain by twisting; *torment*, inflicting psychological pain that would be comparable to the physical pain of, say, twisting an arm or worse; and *torque*, "rotational force."

What we don't get from *torquere* is *tornado*, at least not directly. *Tornado* comes from the Spanish *tronada*, "thunderstorm," from the Latin *tonare*, "to thunder," also the root of *astonish*. Presumably, such a storm was called *tronada* because those who named it were more impressed by the storm's noise than by its twisting two hundred mile-per-hour winds.

But later, influenced by an existing Spanish word, *tornar*, "to twist," the letters *ro* of *tronado's* first syllable were reversed, becoming *or*. This kind of letter shifting is called "metathesis." And how appropriate that this linguistic process would twist *tronado* into *tornado*.

tradition & treason

Although young people, anarchists, and avant-garde artists frequently rail against tradition, most people value at least some of the wisdom and practices handed down from past generations. Indeed, even the act of protesting against tradition has a long tradition.

On the other hand, you can search long and hard without finding a positive word on behalf of treason or the perpetrators of the act, traitors such as Benedict Arnold and Vidkun Quisling.

It's shocking then that *tradition* and *treason* come from the same source. *Tradition* entered English in the fourteenth century via an old French word, *tradicion*, from the Latin *tradere*, a compound of *trans-*, "over," and *dare*, "to give." Figuratively, *tradere* meant "to pass on," an idea at the core the modern word *tradition*.

Treason is from the Old French *traison*, also from *tradere*. However, influenced by another French word, *trair*, "betray," *traison* referred to giving documents to the enemy.

Through metaphorical extension, *treason* came to name betrayal in nongovernmental circumstances. So for example, the celebrated football coach John Heisman could say, "To break training without permission is an act of treason." And T. S. Eliot could write: "The last temptation is the great treason: to do the right deed for the wrong reason."

twig & twelve

The etymological link binding *twig* and *twelve* is subtle but wonderful. Here's a clue: the Old English word for *twig*—*twigge*—didn't mean a small branch but rather a branch that forked off another branch. In essence, you needed two branches for something to be a twig.

This should give away the fact that twig's etymology goes back to a hypothetical Indo-European root *dwo*, "two," from which we also get *twins*, *twine* (two threads), *between* (said of one thing located in relationship to two other things), *twilight*, and—according to some experts—*twist* (from the process of spinning two strands of yarn into a single thread).

That's the easy part of the pair. But *twelve*? The *tw* looks two-ish, but how does *twelve*'s meaning—a dozen—square with *two*? Etymologists explain that *twelve* is actually an ancient compound constructed from *dwo*, "two," plus *lif*, the source of *leave*. The idea is that twelve equals ten with two left over—that is ten plus two. This somewhat twisted hypothesis is given credibility by an analysis of *eleven*, which can be traced back to a compound of *ain*, "one," plus *lif*, in other words, one left over from ten.

It might have been simpler if the number namers had just been a bit more consistent and—using the model of numbers thirteen through nineteen—called *eleven* "one-teen" and *twelve* "two-teen." (In case this idea catches on, remember where you read it first.)

Interestingly, elementary school kids are trained in the same sort of ancient number splitting when learning their number facts. For example, they may learn to add "11 + 8" by regrouping so that the problem becomes "(10 + 1) + 8." No one tells the math students that they're learning an ancient thought process.

umbrage & umbrella

Even the most casual look at *umbrage* and *umbrella* suggests that the two words are linked. But with the former meaning "offense" and the latter referring to a piece of rain gear, the connection is a bit obscure. As it happens, obscurity is what these two words are all about.

Umbrage comes from the Middle French *ombrage*, "shade, shadow," which traces back to the Latin *umbra*, of the same meaning. By the seventeenth century, through metaphorical extension, *umbrage* had acquired the meaning of "being left in the dark," which lead to the sense of "resentment." In our time, *umbrage* has become a linguistic one-trick pony. In ordinary discourse it is rarely used outside the stock phrase "to take umbrage at," that is, to "resent."

Umbrella entered English as a modification of the Italian *ombrello*, from the Latin *umbella*, a diminutive of *umbra*, meaning "sunshade." You are, literally, giving yourself a little shadow. The idea is perhaps clearer in the synonym *parasol*, from the Latin *para*, "protection from," plus *sol*, "sun."

In northern regions, the umbrella inevitably came to be used more often as a means of protection from the rain. The French recognized this fact, which is why the modern French word for umbrella is *parapluie*, the element *pluie* meaning "rain."

Were the English too set in their ways to rename the umbrella something like "rain shield" or were they just hoping against hope that the sun would come out?

vacant & vacation

When you're on vacation, do you sometimes find yourself lying on your back and staring in a vacant way up at the clouds? If so, that makes sense etymologically as well as recreationally.

Both *vacant* and *vacation* come to English from the Latin *vacare* meaning "empty." The *vacuum* in *vacuum cleaner* traces back to the same Latin verb. By creating a partial vacuum, the device causes air to flow into the tube, bringing dirt with it. But all this sounds too much like work, and our focus here is on the opposite.

As early as the fourteenth century, *vacation* meant "freedom from work or work-like occupations, such as attending school." By emptying ourselves of the ordinary chores of everyday life, we have the opportunity to re-create ourselves. So the next time you're on a driving vacation and come to a motel with a flashing "vacancy" sign, it could be a good omen.

But that's just the beginning of the path toward renewal. As Arnold Toynbee wrote, "To be able to fill leisure intelligently is the last product of civilization."

vegetarian & vigilant

Although many scientific authorities have gathered evidence that a vegetarian diet has strong health benefits, the great majority of vegetarians pursue their dietary practices for religious or ethical reasons. They believe that their approach is one of enlightenment. Etymology supports this point of view.

Vegetarian goes back through the Old French *vegetable*, "fit to live," to the Latin *vegetare*, "to enliven." This Latin verb, which is the parent of *vigor*, "to flourish," traces back further to a hypothetical Indo-European root *weg*, "be strong, lively."

Ethics enters the picture when we learn that *weg* also has a spiritual dimension. It is, for example, the source of the Old English *wacan*, "to wake up, to arise," and it also gave rise to the Latin *vigilia*, "watchfulness," from which English gets *vigilant*, "wakefulness," which can be seen as a synonym for enlightenment.

So even if you enjoy steak, if you want nirvana, eat five servings of fruits and vegetables every day, or is it now seven servings?

vicar & vicarious

I conducted a small experiment that showed that the two words most often associated with *vicarious* are *pleasures* and *thrills*. *Vicarious* suggests second-hand experiences, gained, for example, through reading or watching movies. None of my experimental subjects saw a connection between *vicarious* and *vicar* yet the two are kissing cousins, etymologically speaking.

Vicar, the older of the pair, comes from the Old French *vicaire*, which traces back to the Latin *vicarius*, "substitute." In the fourteenth century, the word was used to name a layperson functioning as a substitute and handling the duties of the parish priest as if actually ordained.

Vicarious came from the Latin root *vicarious*, and we see the meaning of "substitute" in the phrase "vicarious punishment" that is meted out when one person stands in for another. A famous example is the hero of *A Tale of Two Cities* going to the guillotine in the place of another man.

Gradually, the sense of "as if" extended the meaning of *vicarious* so that it came to label feelings a person experienced as if he or she were in a different situation. Thus, instead of being an actual substitute, the substitution was imaginary. It is this sense that provides the foundation for Aristotle's belief that drama can allow members of an audience to undergo catharsis while watching the sufferings of a character on stage.

villa & villain

Although vile characters such as Lady Macbeth and Jack the Ripper make perfect villains, etymologically *vile* and *villain* are unconnected. While *vile* and its companion *vilify* trace back to the Latin *vilis*, "cheap, worthless," *villain* is of the manor born.

Villa comes to English from the Latin *villa*, "country estate." In the Middle Ages, a person who was a servant on the estate was called a "villain." The word at first simply related the person to the place, just as *villager* is defined as someone who lives in a village, which itself ultimately comes from *villa*.

The estate owners, however, came to see villains—especially those who worked in the fields—as lower-class boors or louts. It was only a step from such condescending terms to applying the term *villain* to people who were not merely unrefined, but downright disagreeable or even wicked.

Now it turns out that modern-day villains often have the trappings of the upper class. Think of the mansions of Goldfinger or Tony Soprano or the folks who turned *Enron* into a synonym for scandal.

Thus, those neighbors living in the $5 million villa just up the street from you might prove to be the real villains even if they never get their hands dirty.

virtual reality & virtue

We can't end this book without addressing the issue of gender bias in language. The words above give us a perfect opportunity to do so.

Virtual reality refers to digital images that seem real. Although best known in the context of computer games, VR (as those in the know label it) has serious applications. Simulations permit people to practice difficult and even dangerous activities, such as overcoming phobias, guiding spacecraft, and developing surgical skills.

The phrase is new, but the idea goes back at least to Plato, who—in his celebrated parable attacking representational art—described cave dwellers who foolishly took the shadows on the wall to be real. Because we are so much more sophisticated than Plato's characters, we can skip the etymology of *reality* and focus on *virtual*, from the Latin *virtus*, figuratively, "excellent, strength," and literally, "manliness." *Virtus* goes back to *vir*, "man," the source of virtue, and its relative *virtuoso*.

Even a thousand years ago, males had no monopoly on *virtue* and its kin. But we can guess the sex of the wordsmiths who coined those words.

Starting in the 1960s, feminists led the campaign to replace sex-stereotyped words. Thus, *fireman* became *firefighter*, *stewardess* became *flight attendant*, and *businessman* became *entrepreneur* or *executive*. These modest changes contributed to the democratization of opportunity.

Because few people have had enough Latin to recognize the bias in the *vir-* words discussed here, perhaps they need not be replaced. After all, in the real reality—as opposed to the virtual kind—who has ever objected to calling a virtuous woman *virtuous* or an accomplished woman a *virtuoso*?

wash & wishy-washy

Just as movies are not shot in chronological order, *Words of a Feather* wasn't written in alphabetical order. I thought about this piece early on but, because I wasn't sure it belonged, I kept putting it off.

Was it profound enough for the discriminating reader of this volume? Maybe not, yet on the other hand the word does have a nice sound. Of course, the book already contained one reduplication—*flimflam*—so perhaps this would be seen as redundant. Maybe *redundant* would make a better entry. But if I didn't include *wishy-washy* it would be a waste of the research already done. I guess I could put *wishy-washy* on my gravestone. Naw, better to use it now.

The experts agree—quite firmly, actually—that the base of *wishy-washy* is *wash*, from the Old English *wascan*, which traces back to the hypothetical Indo-European root *wed*, "water, wet." *Wed-* is the source of *vodka*, and maybe we need an entry about that. Or maybe not.

Anyway, *wash* originally referred to washing clothes. The Old English had a completely different verb for the action of washing the body, which some sources say rarely happened.

As for how *wishy-washy* came into existence, perhaps it had to do with the notion of something being watery, not substantial, not firm. Or maybe the base really was *wishy*—from the Old English *wyscan*, "desire"— and the notion of consigning yourself to whatever fate might bring.

Or maybe . . .

work & wrought

Although *work* is one of the most commonly used words—though not always with positive feelings—its close relative *wrought* is relatively obscure. Yet in 1837 *wrought* figured in one of the most historic messages ever sent. For his first public demonstration of the telegraph, Samuel Morse typed the words "What hath God wrought," borrowed from the King James Version of the Bible.

Wrought is the Middle English past particle of the word *work*. In the old days, it was used to form the past tense, which is now expressed by *worked*. A few similar Middle English past particles are still in use, for example *caught*, *fought*, and *taught*. Whether these will ever be "regularized" into *catched*, *fighted*, and *teached* remains to be seen. But for now, there are just two contemporary uses of *wrought*: in the adjective *overwrought* (*overworked*) and the phrase *wrought iron*, meaning iron that has been worked on—hammered—by a blacksmith.

Work is from Old English, one of those trusty four-letter words that never seem to die. Etymologists have traced it back to its hypothetical Indo-European root *werg*, "to do," which spawned numerous modern English words include *energy*, *organ*, and *orgy*.

That last word may surprise some people, who don't associate work with sensual happenings. But we must remember the words of Baudelaire, known in part for his erotic poetry: "It is necessary to work, if not from inclination, at least from despair. Everything considered, work is less boring than amusing oneself."

xylem &xylophone

Names of musical instruments have varied etymologies. For example, the name may come from the instrument's shape (*triangle*), its inventor's name (*saxophone* from Antoine-Joseph Sax), its volume (*piano* shortened from *pianoforte*—soft and loud), or its structure (*sitar* from an Old Persian word meaning "three-stringed").

Xylophone is named for its wood bars of various lengths which, when struck, produce notes of the chromatic scale. The first part of the word—*xylon*—comes from the Greek for "wood." The same Greek word is the source of *xylem*, "the woody cells in a tree that transport water and minerals from the ground to the leaves."

If the bars of a xylophone are made of substances other than wood, purists give the instrument a different name, for example *metallophones* (bars made of metal) or *lithophones* (bars made of rocks).

The second part of the word is also Greek—*phone*—meaning "sound, voice, speak." Appearing unchanged in words such as *telephone* and *phonetics*, through a long and twisty path, *phone* also gave rise to *fame*, the meaning coming from the notion that famous people are much talked about.

yoga & yoke

Of the many inventions credited to the Indian people—including the university, the heliocentric model, trigonometry, and the scientific study of language—yoga is among the best known. Certainly it engages a huge and diverse number of practitioners on a regular basis.

Now often treated as a technique for achieving physical fitness, yoga originated as a means to gain enlightenment, and its name reflects its origins. In the early nineteenth century, *yoga* entered English unchanged from the Hindi *yoga*, which traces back to a Sanskrit word meaning "union." Implicit was "union with the Supreme Spirit."

Etymologists have traced *yoga* further back to a hypothetical Proto-Indo-European root *yeug*, "to join." The same root, via the Latin *iungere*, "to join," gave rise to many modern English expressions that involve the sense of connecting. A few examples are: *joint*, *junction*, *junta*, *conjunction*, and *jugular*.

Yoke is another one of these "joining" words, coming from the Old English *geoc*. While literally a frame with loops to harness a pair of oxen together, as with *yoga*, *yoke* has long been used in spiritual metaphors, as in this Biblical quotation: "Take my yoke upon you, and learn of me; for I am meek and lowly in heart; and you shall find rest for your souls."

zodiac & zoo

Although we live in the age of science and technology, a huge number of people value the ancient (and perpetually unproven) practice of astrology. Studies show that about 15 percent of college undergraduates believe in astrology, while nearly 40 percent of adults accept it as scientific. No wonder that two-thirds of U.S. daily newspapers print horoscopes, while thousands of astrologers earn their livings from the stars. Conclusion? If word lovers hold the same views, this will be a very popular entry.

Zodiac comes—through French and Latin—from the Greek word *zodiakos*, derived from *zoion*, "animal," and *kyklos*, "circle." Thus *zodiakos* is a "circle of little carved animals," which refers to the twelve constellations that astrologers consulted for information about past, present, and future events. (However, in western astrology not all the constellations took the form of animals.)

Meanwhile back on earth, people had long been collecting exotic creatures. The first modern facility devoted to the scientific investigation of animals opened in London in 1828. It was known as the Zoological Gardens of the London Zoological Society, the word *zoological* tracing back to the Latin *zoologia*, a compound of *zoo*, "animal," plus *logia*, "study." *Zoo* in turn goes back to the Greek *zoion*, "animal," which we learned was the source of *zodiakos*.

While zoological refers to animals that often seem to be curiosities, a curiosity of *zoological* is that it is one of the most frequently mispronounced words in the English language. The word is spoken in five syllables: zo o log i cal—the first syllable rhyming with "go."

zodiac & zoo

Word Factory

No one knows for sure how human beings first acquired language. Was our species hard-wired to invent language or was speech an accidental discovery—one ape's angry grunt at some point suddenly understood by another ape?

What we do know is that eventually words came to be produced in more than a dozen of ways. Some are common, such as joining two old words together to make a new one: *airplane*, *doughnut*, *superman*. Others are more unusual, such as merging only parts of two words to make a new one—*smoke* plus *fog* giving us *smog*.

Throughout *Words of a Feather* we refer in passing to a number of these word-making processes. This section provides definitions and additional examples. The information is meant not only to enrich your enjoyment of this book but also to be useful

when you are using dictionaries and other resources to explore
etymologies on your own.

Acronyms

An acronym is a word formed from the first letter or first few letters of several words or syllables within words. Unlike an initial
word, in which the name of each letter is pronounced (*FBI* = ef
bee eye), an acronym is pronounced as a single word. For example, *AWOL* (from absent without leave) is pronounced "a-wall."
Other examples include:

- *radar* from *radio detecting and ranging*
- *NASA* from *National Aeronautics and Space
  Administration*
- *RAM* from *random access memory*
- *scuba* from *self-contained underwater breathing apparatus*
- *ZIP* code from *zone improvement plan*

Yuppie, a Reagan-era coinage, is a more complex version of
this type: the first syllable—*yup*—is an acronym from young,
upwardly mobile professional; the second syllable—*pie*—is a suffix that makes the word diminutive, connoting contempt.

Back-Formations

It's common for one word to spawn another word used as a different part of speech—for example, *run* (a verb) giving rise to
runner (a noun). Generally, the new word is longer.

With a back-formation, the newer word is usually shorter and appears to be the source word. As in the following list, back-formations are often verbs made from nouns. Some examples:

- *babysit* from *babysitter*
- *burgle* from *burglar*
- *cremate* from *cremation*
- *emote* from *emotion*
- *fixate* from *fixation*
- *jell* from *jelly*
- *negate* from *negation*

However, you may encounter instances of nouns back-formed from adjectives (*telepath* from *telepathic*) and adjectives back-formed from nouns (*surreal* from *surrealism*). Author Joseph Shipley created the back-formation *back-formed* (used in the previous sentence) as a witty example of this type of word.

Blends

Also known as *portmanteau words*, blends are a subcategory of compound words (treated below). The difference is that with a blend only part of each contributing word is used. Lewis Carroll may have originated this type or at least popularized it with coinages such as *galumph* from *gallop* and *triumph*. Less literary examples include:

- *brunch* from *breakfast* plus *lunch*
- *Interpol* from *international* plus *police*
- *motel* from *motor* plus *hotel*
- *sitcom* from *situation* plus *comedy*

Borrowed Words

The great majority of English words began in other languages and were usually changed in structure by the time they settled into English. So, for example, *science* came from the Latin *scientia*. Much of etymology deals with tracing a borrowed word's development from Modern English back through its various forms found in one or perhaps many other languages.

Within the category of borrowed words is a subcategory known as *loan words*. These words remained mostly unchanged in terms of spelling and pronunciation. In a sense, they are like immigrants who maintain their culture while living in a new land. Usually, it's easy to identify the lending language.

Many foods fit in this loan group:

- *biscotti* (Italian)
- *chow mein* (Chinese)
- *sangria* (Spanish)
- *vodka* (Russian)

Some noncomestible examples of loan words are:

- *angst* (German)
- *armoire* (French)
- *deus ex machina* (Latin)
- *habeas corpus* (Latin)
- *ipso facto* (Latin)
- *kibitz* (Yiddish)
- *kindergarten* (German)
- *sombrero* (Spanish)

Coinages

Although logic tells us that *every* word was used for the first time by one person—the originator—usually that person's identity is unknown, especially when the word was created in the distant past.

The term *coinage* refers to a word whose inventor—a specific person or organization—is known. Examples include:

- *blurb*—coined in 1907 by humorist Gelett Burgess
- *dashiki*—coined in 1967 by its manufacturer J. Benning
- *pandemonium*—coined in 1667 by John Milton as the name of Satan's palace

The great majority of coinages are made by scientists naming things in nature (plants, animals, elements, etc.) and by corporations naming their proprietary products. In the latter case, the names are usually trademarked, a legal action that restricts how the words may be used.

Compounds

Compound words are made by joining two earlier words: *overcoat* from *over* plus *coat*; *touchdown* from *touch* plus *down*.

Compounding is one of the most frequently used word-creating methods. In most cases, the etymology is easy to figure out. But sometimes, because of pronunciation or spelling changes, the meaning of one or both of the original words is obscured. An example is *breakfast*, with the first word being pronounced "brek." Of course, the spelling is a visual reminder of what the compound actually means (breaking of a period of fasting).

Cupboard is another example. The pronunciation "cubboard" hides the fact that the word was coined to name a place for storing cups. The fact that we now keep many other things in a cupboard—often none of them cups—takes us farther away from the etymology.

Among etymologists, the most infamous "disguised compound" is *woman*. The Old English compound came from *wif*, "a female" plus *mann*, "a human being" (**not** "a man"). Changes in spelling led to the mistaken idea that this is a sexist term.

A more current example is the use of *gate* in various compounds. The scandal that ended Richard Nixon's presidency began with a break-in at the Watergate office and apartment complex in Washington, DC. The crime eventually became known as "Watergate." Although the "gate" in Watergate originally referred to a device for controlling water in a canal, in this case "gate" took on the meaning of "scandal." Thus, when the next huge political contretemps occurred—involving the illegal sale of arms to Iran—some journalistic wordsmith dubbed it *Irangate*. Which was followed by President Clinton's *Monicagate*. Which will be followed by . . .

Contractions

One of the most prolific word-making processes is *contraction*, also known as *abbreviation*, *clipping*, and *shortening*. This method involves dropping one or more letters or syllables from a single word or from a phrase or in some cases dropping an entire word from a phrase. Examples include:

- *hi-def* from *high-definition*
- *homer* from *home run*
- *lunch* from *luncheon*
- *pants* from *pantaloons*
- *principal* from *principal teacher*

The location of the omitted letters may be indicated by an apostrophe:

- *o'clock* from *of the clock*
- *'sup* from *what's up*
- *'tude* from *attitude*
- *y'all* from *you all*

Some dictionaries use parentheses to indicate clipping:

- *bus* < (*omni*)*bus*
- *exam* < *exam*(*ination*)

With abbreviations, a period is often used. Sometimes the pronunciation is unchanged—*Dr.* pronounced as "doc-tor." In other cases—known as *initial words*—only the letters will be pronounced, with the original words forgotten by many speakers—for example, A.M. for *ante meridiem*, meaning "before noon."

Derived Words

Derivation—adding prefixes and suffixes—is one of the most common word-making methods. Such "erector-set" words are formed by adding elements (affixes) to base words or roots. There are two kinds of affixes: prefixes and suffixes.

A prefix is a syllable or a group of syllables attached to the front of a word:

original word	*think*
prefix	*re-*
derived word	*rethink*

A suffix is a syllable or a group of syllables attached to the end of a word:

original word	*free*
suffix	*-dom* (state of being)
derived word	*freedom*

Note that affixes cannot stand by themselves: *re-* and *-dom* are not independent words. If an independent word is attached to a word, then the result is called a compound word: *pin* + *head* = *pinhead*.

It is possible to add more than one affix to a word. For example, *unrepentant* has two prefixes (*un-* and *re-*) and one suffix (*-ant*).

Diminutives

The slogan for this section might be "think small." A diminutive is a word formed from another word by adding a suffix that conveys the idea of small size, affection, or cuteness. Often the original word is in plain view:

- *Annie* from *Ann*
- *booklet* from *book*

- *cigarette* from *cigar*
- *duckling* from *duck*
- *kitty* from *kitten*
- *kitchenette* from *kitchen*
- *manikin* from *man*
- *quickie* from *quick*

In other cases, the original word has disappeared from current use or is from another language:

- *jacket* from *jack*, a medieval soldier's sleeveless coat
- *marionette* from *Marion*, a given name
- *pocket* from *poque*, French for "pouch"
- *puppet* from *poupe*, French for "doll"

Euphemisms

Although some people believe that there are no "bad" words, the reality is that many people find certain words shocking, irreverent, insulting, obscene, or embarrassing. This isn't a matter merely of taste. Using certain taboo words over the public airways can result in a huge fine. At work, it can mean the loss of employment. In an election campaign, it can hand victory to the other side.

Enter euphemism, the art of substituting an acceptable synonym for a possibly controversial word in order to keep people from thinking about something they don't want to think about. Commonly used types of euphemisms include:

- abbreviation: S.O.B. for *son of a bitch*
- changed spelling and pronunciation: *darn* for *damn*
- description: *white meat* for *chicken breast*, *backside* for *ass*

- baby talk: *poop* for *shit*
- indirect reference: *passing on* for *died*

Sometimes two or more euphemisms will stand between the audience and reality. For example: *men's* is a contraction of *men's room*, which is a descriptive synonym for *room with toilets*, which . . .

Folk Etymologies

Words in this section are the opposite of loan words, discussed earlier. Through a process technically known as *folk etymology*, native speakers, who don't accurately hear the way a foreign word is pronounced, change the pronunciation so that one or more of its parts sound like familiar syllables. The transformation obscures the word's link to its etymological roots. Some examples:

- *Cockroach* comes from the Spanish *cucaracha*, with *cuca* referring to "a type of insect." English speakers turned *cuca* into *cock*, "rooster." It didn't make "sense," but the word became part of the language.
- *Gingerbread* comes from an Old French word *gingerbras*, "preserved ginger." The syllable *bras* meant nothing in English, so when ginger was baked into a kind of cake, the result perhaps suggested the notion of bread. Eventually *gingerbras* became *gingerbread*, although no one thinks of it as bread.
- *Wedlock* comes from the Old English *wedlac*, a compound of wed, "a pledge," and *lac*, "a gift." Perhaps the notion that a married couple were "locked" together changed *lac* into *lock*.

When foreign words are folk etymologized into English, this is called *anglicizing*. The same process goes on in every language that imports words.

Something similar occurs with *mondegreens*, the mishearing of song lyrics. For example, to many listeners Jimi Hendrix's phrase "'Scuse me while I kiss the sky" sounded like "'Scuse me while I kiss this guy."

Imitative Words

English is filled with hundreds of words that imitate sounds: *bang*, *buzz*, *clang*, *clatter*, *crash*, *drip*, *grunt*, *hum*, *meow*, *mumble*, *oink*, *poop*, *splash*, *tap*, *thump*, *tinkle*, and *whir*. Depending on the dictionary or reference you use, such words may be called *echoic* (echoing nature) or *onomatopoetic*.

Imitative words not only name sounds but also objects that make the sounds—for example, *buzzer*, *flip-flops*, and *gong*.

Interestingly, people speaking different languages often represent the same natural sounds with very different words. While an English speaker will describe the following familiar animal cries like this—*cock-a-doodle-do* and *arf-arf*—a French speaker uses *coquerico* for the rooster's crow and the Arabic speaker *haw-haw* for the dog bark. Linguists have theorized that the people speaking different languages actually hear sounds differently.

Initial Words

Initial words are an extreme type of contraction made up of the first letter of each word in a phrase. Unlike acronyms (treated above), the name of each letter is spoken—for example, *C.O.D.* is pronounced "see oh dee"). Periods may or may not follow each letter:

- A.M. from *amplitude modulation*, a type of radio signal
- U.S.A.
- BLT from *bacon, lettuce, and tomato sandwich*
- FBI from *Federal Bureau of Investigation*
- CSI from *crime scene investigation*
- HIV from *human immunodeficiency virus*
- R.B.I. from *runs batted in*
- RSVP from the French *repondez s'il vous plait*, "please reply"

CD-ROM is a mixed form, the first half being an initial word pronounced "see-dee" and derived from "compact disk" and the second half being an acronym pronounced "rom" and derived from "read only memory."

Metathetic Alterations

Metathesis is the formation of a word by switching around the letters found in an earlier word. Examples include:

- *crud* from *curd*
- *curl* from *crullen*
- *omelet* from *alemette*
- *third* from *thrid*
- *trouble* from *turbula*

Metathesis is usually an accidental process. A current example is the pronunciation "ekcetera" for the phrase *et cetera*. But this means of word production has been used deliberately with humorous intent, as with the creation of *sideburns*, an alteration of the last name of Union general Ambrose Everett Burnside.

Name Words

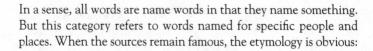

In a sense, all words are name words in that they name something. But this category refers to words named for specific people and places. When the sources remain famous, the etymology is obvious:

- *Christianity*
- *mickey mouse* (meaning "childish" or "simplistic")
- *napoleon* (the pastry)
- *Washington, DC*

But often, the connection will be obscure either because we are unfamiliar with the source:

- *braille* from Louis Braille
- *mesmerize* from F. A. Mesmer, a physician who experimented with hypnosis
- *sadism* from the Marquis de Sade
- *tantalize* named for a mythical Greek king, Tantalus
- *tuxedo* named for a country club in Tuxedo Park, New York
- *utopia* named for a fictional place in a novel by Thomas More

Or because the original name was garbled when it came into English:

- *currant*, a type of raisin grown in *Corinth*
- *denim*, a type of fabric made in *de Nimes*
- *jeans*, a type of fabric made in *Genoa*

Reduplications

A reduplication is a playful word made up of two elements that rhyme or have similar sounds. One part, called the *base*—which can be at the front or the back—often has a recognizable meaning. The other part typically is a nonsense word added for emphasis or just for the fun of it. Examples include:

- *fiddle-faddle*
- *hanky-panky*
- *heebie-jeebies*
- *mumbo-jumbo*
- *nitty-gritty*
- *ping-pong*
- *pitter-patter*
- *razzle-dazzle*
- *shilly-shally*
- *teeny-weeny*
- *walkie-talkie*

Semantically Changed Words

Many words retain their structure but acquire new meanings. In doing so, they become new words. A good example is *plastic*.

Originally the word meant "something moldable," but with the development of polymers, it came also to mean the hard substance after it is molded, a meaning that seems to be the opposite of *plastic*.

Similarly, *nice* once meant "difficult to please, fastidious," but now its synonyms tend to be words like *pleasant*, *polite*, and *fine*.

Metaphorical thinking also helps transform words. For example, originally a *smoke screen* was literally a cloud of smoke spread to hide military maneuvers. That meaning has disappeared and the phrase now suggests any action taken to conceal or mislead.

Words are constantly changing, which is perhaps what motivated Lewis Carroll to write the following in *Through the Looking Glass*:

> "I don't know what you mean by 'glory,'" Alice said.
>
> Humpty Dumpty smiled contemptuously. "Of course you don't—till I tell you. I meant 'there's a nice knock-down argument for you!'"
>
> "But 'glory' doesn't mean 'a nice knock-down argument,'" Alice objected.
>
> "When I use a word," Humpty Dumpty said in a rather scornful tone, "it means just what I choose it to mean—neither more or less."
>
> "The question is," said Alice, "whether you can make words mean so many different things."
>
> "The question is," said Humpty Dumpty, "which is to be master—that's all."

Resources

I consulted many resources while writing *Words of a Feather*. The following were those that were the most important. I recommend them to anyone who wishes to study and/or write about words.

Books

Dictionary of Word Origins by John Ayto (Arcade/Little Brown, 1990)

Ayto gives clearly written, wonderfully detailed etymologies of more than eight thousand words. Almost every entry includes doublets.

In Praise of English: The Growth and Use of Language by Joseph T. Shipley (Times Books, 1977)

This classic covers the origins of language, methods of word development, semantics, synonyms, antonyms, homonyms, slang, euphemism, poetry, prose, literary forms, symbolism, and diction. It's an entertaining way to acquire a background in word study.

Word Origins: An Exploration and History of Words and Language by Wilfred Funk (Wings Books, 1950)

Unlike Ayto, who uses an alphabetical organization, Funk groups words into interesting categories, such as the boudoir, emotions, business, home, garden, dining, animals, politics, and war.

Word Origins and How We Know Them by Anatoly Liberman (Oxford, 2005)

While this book gives fascinating etymologies of hundreds of words, its main purpose is to take the reader inside the head of a highly skilled—and extremely witty—etymologist. The book's motto is "Etymology for Everyone." That might be a bit over-reaching. The book is sophisticated and challenging. But it will surely educate and delight everyone who loves words.

Websites

Bartleby.com
www.bartleby.com

The site calls itself "The preeminent Internet publisher of literature, reference and verse, providing students, researchers and the intellectually curious with unlimited access to books and information on the web, free of charge."

The site's reference area includes *American Heritage Dictionary, Fourth Edition* (incredibly helpful for etymological research), *Bartlett's Familiar Quotations, Columbia Encyclopedia, Sixth Edi-*

tion, King James Bible, The Oxford Shakespeare, and *Roget's II: The New Thesaurus*.

Expressions & Sayings
http://users.tinyonline.co.uk/gaswithenbank/sayindex.htm

This is the best source we've found for the origins of familiar expressions and sayings, such as "gild the lily," "gung-ho, "go to hell in a hand basket," "pin money," and "pot calling the kettle black." The site was built in the United Kingdom and thus has some phrases that may not be familiar to Americans.

Online Etymology Dictionary
www.etymonline.com

This remarkable site—created by historian-author-journalist Douglas Harper—offers thousands of easily accessible etymologies. As a valuable bonus, for each word that you call up, the site provides a list of words related by origin and/or meaning. In effect, you get a thesaurus-cum-etymological dictionary.

Access is free and there are no annoying ads. To help support the site, you can "sponsor" words at the modest cost of $10. This venture is definitely worth supporting.

Quotations Page
www.quotationspage.com

Many of the quotations used to illustrate *Words of a Feather* came from this easy-to-use network of quotation sites.

Wikipedia
www.wikipedia.org

This is the place I turn to for facts, fact checking, and entertaining reading when I need a break.

About the Author

Murray Suid, M.F.A., has written more than two dozen books including *How to Be President of the U.S.A.*, *Demonic Mnemonics*, and *The Kids' How to Do (Almost) Everything Guide*. A former writing instructor at San Jose State University, he developed content for software products including *Oval Office* and *Launch: The New Millennium Business Game*. A screenwriter, he recently started Point Reyes Pictures, an independent movie company. He lives in Inverness, California.